Your

Final

Third

An Enlightening Guide to
Thriving in Retirement

Don Hastings

Connect with Don Hastings at www.seniorsolutionstoday.com

Published by Edumarketing www.edumarketing.com

About the Author:

Don Hastings is a seasoned entrepreneur and financial expert with a mission to simplify the often-overwhelming world of retirement planning. With a career spanning multiple industries—including healthcare, wellness & fitness, insurance, real estate, and personal development—Don has built a wealth of knowledge, all of which he now channels into helping others thrive in their later years.

A Registered Social Security Analyst (RSSA), Don's unique expertise lies in demystifying the complexities of Social Security and Medicare, ensuring that retirees maximize their benefits and make informed financial decisions. Through his company, *Senior Solutions Today*, he has made it his life's work to help retirees navigate the often-confusing maze of retirement options, government programs, and financial planning strategies.

Don's journey to becoming a trusted retirement advisor is deeply personal. After a successful career in various sectors, he found himself, like many others, perplexed by the intricacies of retirement planning. Determined to not only master these complexities but also to share his knowledge, Don created *Senior Solutions Today* as a resource for those facing similar challenges. Along the way, he earned additional certifications and sharpened his skills in Social Security optimization, real estate for retirees, and insurance strategies, particularly focused on securing a stable future for those in their "final third" of life.

As a real estate broker, Don understands the pivotal role housing decisions play in retirement. Whether it's downsizing, relocating, or investing in income-generating properties, Don offers insightful advice tailored to meet the needs of retirees seeking comfort and financial stability in their new phase of life. His work as an insurance agency principal ensures his clients are well-protected, with comprehensive estate planning, wills, trusts, and essential insurance products, all designed to secure their wealth and protect their legacies for future generations.

In addition to his financial acumen, Don is a certified Personal Development & Fitness Coach, understanding that retirement is not just about money—it's about living life to its fullest. He integrates wellness and personal development into his retirement strategies, encouraging clients to maintain physical fitness, mental agility, and a positive mindset as they transition into this exciting phase of life.

As a passionate advocate for financial literacy, Don serves as a Financial Literacy Educator with the *Society for Financial Awareness* (SOFA), working to end financial illiteracy across America. Through workshops, seminars, and personalized coaching, Don has touched the lives of many, helping them understand the importance of early preparation and strategic financial planning.

In *Your Final Third: An Enlightening Guide to Thriving in Retirement*, Don combines his vast experience, certifications, and personal journey to offer readers a roadmap to a successful and fulfilling retirement. He presents practical, actionable strategies that go beyond financial advice, encompassing personal development, health, and social connections. His comprehensive approach ensures that retirees not only survive but *thrive* during their golden years.

Whether you're approaching retirement or already in it, Don's engaging and easy-to-understand writing offers valuable insights, reflection exercises, and tools that empower readers to take control of their retirement. This book is designed to be more than just a guide; it's a trusted companion on the journey toward a rewarding, healthy, and financially secure "final third."

For more insights and resources, connect with Don Hastings at:

www.seniorsolutionstoday.com.

Foreword

If you are reading this, it is quite likely that despite having managed your life well up to this point, you find yourself being intimidated, frustrated, and/or confused by all this "Retirement Stuff", especially the ever-changing world of Social Security and Medicare.

Well, join the club my friend, for even after years of multi-industry entrepreneurship (including Healthcare, Fitness, Insurance, Finance, Real Estate and Personal Development), thanks to the countless rules, regulations, acronyms, and hearsay from pundits supposedly "in the know", I found myself in the same boat in a "sea of complexity and confusion".

So, I took it upon myself to "un-retire", dig into all these rules, regulations, and acronyms, educate myself further on Social Security and Medicare (picking up a few more certifications along the way), create Senior Solutions Today and during MY "Final Third", commit myself to assisting others to navigate the many complexities of retirement.

Throughout my career (My First Two "Thirds"), I've witnessed firsthand the profound impact that strategic financial planning and informed decision-making, including the process of downsizing and relocating, can have on one's quality of life in retirement; every aspect of the retirement journey is filled with unique challenges as well as some great opportunities.

Today, as a Registered Social Security Analyst, I have the privilege of helping clients maximize and optimize their Social Security benefits and make informed choices about their retirement income. Understanding the intricacies of Social Security, Medicare, and other government benefits is essential for ensuring financial security and peace of mind in retirement.

As a Real Estate Broker, I assist clients in finding the perfect home for their retirement years, whether it's downsizing to a smaller property, relocating to a retirement community, or investing In rental properties for passive income.

As an Insurance Agency Principal, I help clients protect their assets, mitigate risks, and plan for the unexpected.

As a Society of Financial Awareness (SOFA) Financial Literacy Educator, I eagerly answer the call of our mission to end financial illiteracy across America, one community at a time.

And as a Personal Development & Fitness Coach, assisting clients to move from where they are today to where they want to be and truly make their "Retirement Dreams" come true.

In Your Final Third, you'll find a wealth of practical advice, actionable strategies, and expert insights to help you navigate the complexities of retirement planning and embrace your golden years with confidence, excitement, and enthusiasm.

I encourage you to not only _read_ the contents but to get out your highlighters and sticky notes and _learn_ the contents and more importantly _implement_ the contents. At the end of each chapter are Reflection and Review exercises, there are worksheets, checklists and other resources provided throughout which I hope you will take advantage of to enhance your retirement journey.

Whether you're approaching retirement or already enjoying your post-career life, I invite you to embark on this journey of discovery and empowerment.

May this book serve as your trusted companion on the road to a fulfilling and prosperous "Final Third"!

All the best,

Don, "Your Senior Solutions Guy"

Contents

"Retirement is not the end of the road. It's the beginning of a new adventure."

– Unknown

Introduction

This Introduction sets the stage for the rest of the book, emphasizing the positive aspects of aging, the necessity of preparation for the journey ahead, the concept of the "third act" of life and why it's a cause for celebration rather than fear.

Embracing the Third Act

The fact is that none of us really know at what age our "final third" will or did begin. Should you become a centenarian, "mathematically" of course, it will be from age sixty-six and two-thirds to age one hundred and to that I say, "Why not go for it"!

As an early sidebar, if curious about life expectancy, Thomas Perls, MD, MPF, FACP, one of the authors of <u>Living To 100</u>, has an online Life Expectancy Calculator that I have found to be quite thorough. The calculator asks you 40 quick questions related to your health and family history and takes about 10 minutes to complete. Most people score in their late eighties, but you may want to give it a try at www.livingto100.com.

But regardless of the age, as you enter this "third act" of life, you're embarking on what can be the most fulfilling and rewarding chapter yet: "Your Final Third".

This phase is often characterized by retirement, increased leisure time, newfound freedom, wisdom, a shift in priorities and opportunities for personal growth.

 Instead of viewing this stage as a decline or winding down of life, consider it the beginning of a grand finale, filled with possibilities, growth, and self-discovery where you have the chance to embrace new experiences.

Just as a three-act play builds to a climax in its final act, so too can our lives, with the "third act" offering the opportunity for reflection, fulfillment, and the pursuit of passions and legacy.

In this section, we'll explore the concept of the "third act" of life and why it's a time to celebrate rather than fear. By reframing your mindset and embracing the unique opportunities that come with aging, you can set the stage for a fulfilling journey ahead.

Reframing Your Mindset

Aging is a natural and inevitable part of life, and while it may come with its challenges, it also brings unique opportunities for personal growth and enrichment.

By reframing your mindset and adopting a positive outlook on aging, you can shift your focus from limitations to possibilities...from fears to aspirations.

Instead of dwelling on what you may have lost or can no longer do, embrace what you have gained, the wisdom you have accrued, and the freedom to live life on your own terms.

Embracing Unique Opportunities

The "third act" of life offers a wealth of opportunities for exploration, creativity, and self-expression.

With more time and freedom on your hands, you can pursue long-held dreams, explore new hobbies and interests, and deepen connections with loved ones.

Retirement can be seen as a chance to reinvent yourself, to pursue passions that may have been put on hold during your working years, and to make the most of each day.

Setting the Stage for a Fulfilling Journey Ahead

By embracing the "third act" of life with enthusiasm and openness, you can set the stage for a fulfilling and meaningful journey ahead.

Take the time to reflect on your values, aspirations, and goals for this stage of life, and make intentional choices that align with your vision for the future.

Surround yourself with supportive relationships, engage in activities that bring you joy and fulfillment, and cultivate a sense of gratitude for the abundance that life has to offer.

In conclusion, the "third act" of life is not a time to fear or lament, but rather a time to celebrate the richness of experience, the depth of wisdom, and the boundless potential for growth and fulfillment.

By reframing your mindset and embracing the unique opportunities that come with aging, you can set the stage for a truly rewarding journey ahead.

Why Preparation Matters

(The Importance of Early Planning)

This expanded section dives deeper into the importance of preparation for retirement and outlines why it's crucial to start early.

It emphasizes the benefits of early planning, such as building a solid foundation, harnessing the power of compounding, mitigating risks, securing your legacy, and enjoying the journey of anticipation and preparation for retirement.

Understanding and Planning for the "Go Go" ..."Slow Go"..."No Go" Years!

The "Go Go" Years

The "Go Go" years refer to the early phase of retirement, usually from ages 60 to 75, when retirees are generally healthy, active, and eager to enjoy their newfound freedom. During this period, retirees often:

Travel Extensively: Many take advantage of their good health to travel, both domestically and internationally.

Pursue Hobbies: This is a time to dive into hobbies and interests that might have been neglected during their working years.

Stay Physically Active: Regular exercise, sports, and outdoor activities are common as retirees strive to maintain their health.

Socialize: Engaging in social activities, joining clubs, and spending time with family and friends is a priority.

Volunteer: Many find fulfillment in giving back to their communities through volunteer work.

New Ventures: Some retirees might even start new businesses or take on part-time jobs to stay busy and supplement their income.

The "Slow Go" Years

The "Slow Go" years generally occur between ages 75 to 85. During this stage, retirees might begin to experience a decline in energy and health, leading to a slower pace of life. Key characteristics of this period include:

Reduced Travel: While travel is still possible, it might be less frequent and closer to home.

Modified Hobbies: Retirees may continue their hobbies but might choose less physically demanding activities.

Health Management: There is an increased focus on managing health issues and regular medical appointments.

Simplified Living: Some may downsize their homes or move to retirement communities that offer more support.

Financial Adjustments: Spending patterns might change, with a focus on budgeting for healthcare and other essential needs.

Family Time: Spending quality time with children and grandchildren becomes more central.

The "No Go" Years

The "No Go" years typically begin around age 85 and beyond, marked by a decline in physical and sometimes cognitive abilities. During this period, retirees often experience:

Limited Mobility: Many face mobility challenges and may require assistance with daily activities.

Healthcare Needs: There is a greater reliance on healthcare services, possibly including in-home care or assisted living facilities.

Social Engagement: Social activities may decrease but maintaining connections with family and close friends remains important.

Safety and Comfort: Ensuring a safe and comfortable living environment becomes a priority, with modifications to the home or a move to a more supportive setting.

Reflective Time: This is a time for reflection on life, legacy, and spending meaningful moments with loved ones.

Transitioning Between Phases

It's important to note that the transition between these phases is not always clear-cut and can vary greatly among individuals. Factors influencing these transitions include:

Health Status: Chronic illnesses or sudden health issues can accelerate the shift from one phase to another.

Financial Resources: Adequate financial planning can impact the quality of life and the ability to enjoy each phase.

Support System: A strong support network of family and friends can make these transitions smoother and more enjoyable.

Key Milestones and Benefits in the Final Third of Life

Milestone	Age Range	Description	Benefits
Retirement Age	65 years	Transition from work to leisure.	Financial stability, time for hobbies, travel opportunities.
Travel Opportunities	Late 60s to 70s	Exploration and cultural experiences.	Expanded horizons, relaxation, new connections.
Leisure Activities	70s and beyond	Enjoyment of hobbies and community.	Mental stimulation, social engagement, lifelong learning.

Ongoing Preparation Benefits

Area	Benefits
Financial Planning	Security, peace of mind, ability to support loved ones.
Health and Wellness	Active lifestyle, quality of life, reduced medical costs.

Tips for Planning for Each Phase

Financial Planning: Ensure sufficient savings and a well-thought-out budget to cover healthcare and living expenses throughout retirement.

Health Maintenance: Stay proactive about health with regular check-ups, a balanced diet, and exercise.

Social Connections: Cultivate and maintain strong social ties to avoid isolation.

Adaptability: Be prepared to adapt your lifestyle and living arrangements as your needs change.

Legacy Planning: Consider your legacy and make plans for how you want to be remembered, including estate planning and ethical wills.

Thus, preparation is key to making the most of your final third. Just as you meticulously planned for your career, family, and future during your earlier years, it's essential to apply the same level of diligence and foresight to your retirement and beyond.

From financial planning to healthcare decisions to personal development, taking proactive steps now can ensure a smoother transition and a more enjoyable journey ahead.

In the journey of life, preparation is the cornerstone of success, and nowhere is this more evident than in the transition to retirement. As you approach "Your Final Third", diligent preparation becomes not just a prudent choice but a crucial necessity for ensuring a smooth and fulfilling retirement experience.

Whether you're already in retirement or approaching it in the near future, there's no better time than now to lay the groundwork for a fulfilling and prosperous "Final Third".

1. Laying the Groundwork for Success

Preparation is like laying the foundation for a sturdy and resilient home. Just as a strong foundation ensures stability and longevity, early preparation for retirement and the "final third" set the stage for a fulfilling and prosperous future.

By starting early, you have the opportunity to take small, manageable steps over time, gradually building up your resources, knowledge, and support networks to navigate the challenges and opportunities that lie ahead.

A secure and fulfilling retirement rests upon careful financial planning, emotional readiness, and practical preparations. By starting early and laying the groundwork for your retirement years, you set yourself up for greater stability, security, and peace of mind in the years to come.

2. Maximizing Your Resources

Time is one of your most valuable resources when it comes to preparing for retirement. The earlier you start, the more time you have to save and invest for the future, allowing your money to grow through the power of compounding.

Starting early also gives you the opportunity to take advantage of employer-sponsored retirement plans, such as 401(k)s or pension plans, and to make the most of tax-advantaged savings vehicles like IRAs.

By investing your savings wisely and allowing them to grow over time, you can leverage the magic of compounding to exponentially increase your wealth and achieve your long-term financial goals.

So, Harness the Power of Compounding! The earlier you start saving and investing, the more time your money has to grow, resulting in a larger nest egg and greater financial security in retirement.

3. Mitigating Risks and Uncertainties

Life is full of unexpected twists and turns, early preparation allows you to identify, anticipate and mitigate potential risks and uncertainties that may arise in retirement, such as health issues, market volatility, or unexpected expenses.

By building up your savings and establishing a robust financial plan early on, you can create a buffer against unforeseen challenges and uncertainties, providing greater peace of mind and financial security in your later years.

Whether it's health challenges, economic downturns, or unforeseen expenses, having a robust retirement plan in place gives you the flexibility and resilience to weather life's storms and adapt to changing circumstances with confidence and grace.

4. Creating a Lifelong Learning Mindset

Preparation for "Your Final Third" goes beyond just financial planning; it also involves personal development, health and wellness, and social engagement.

Starting early allows you to cultivate a lifelong learning mindset, continuously seeking new knowledge, skills, and experiences that contribute to your overall well-being and fulfillment in retirement.

Whether it's pursuing educational opportunities, staying physically active, or nurturing meaningful relationships, early preparation sets the stage for a vibrant and enriching retirement lifestyle.

5. Seizing Opportunities for Growth and Exploration

Early preparation gives you the freedom and flexibility to explore new opportunities and pursue passions that may have been put on hold during your working years.

Whether it's traveling the world, volunteering for a cause you're passionate about, or starting a new business venture, starting early allows you to embrace the possibilities and make the most of your final third of life.

Enjoying the Journey

Perhaps most importantly, early preparation for retirement allows you to fully embrace the journey and savor the anticipation of the years ahead.

By taking proactive steps to plan for your future, you can alleviate stress, reduce anxiety, and focus on living a fulfilling and purposeful life, knowing that you have laid the groundwork for a bright and prosperous retirement.

Securing Your Legacy

Beyond your own financial security, early preparation for retirement enables you to secure your legacy and provide for your loved ones.

By establishing estate plans, setting up trusts, and making strategic financial decisions, you can ensure that your assets are protected and distributed according to your wishes, leaving a lasting impact for future generations.

In essence, the importance of preparation for retirement cannot be overstated...

By starting early and taking deliberate action to plan for your future, you not only enhance your financial security but also empower yourself to embrace Your Final Third with confidence, optimism, and excitement.

So, seize the opportunity today to lay the foundation for the retirement of your dreams, and embark on a journey of preparation, possibility, and prosperity that will enrich your life for years to come.

In conclusion, the importance of preparation for a fulfilling "Your Final Third" cannot be overstated. By starting early, you maximize your resources, mitigate risks, and create opportunities for growth and exploration.

Reflection and Review

1. What does it mean to embrace the "third act" of life?

Embracing the "third act" refers to approaching retirement and the later stages of life with a positive mindset, viewing them as a new chapter filled with opportunities for growth, fulfillment, and exploration.

2. Why is preparation important for a fulfilling retirement?

Preparation is important because it allows individuals to anticipate and plan for the changes and challenges that come with retirement, ensuring they have the resources, support, and mindset needed to thrive in this new phase of life.

3. What are some common misconceptions or fears about aging and retirement?

Common misconceptions include viewing retirement as a time of decline or loss, fearing financial insecurity or health problems, and underestimating the potential for personal growth and fulfillment in later life.

4. How can reframing your mindset about aging and retirement lead to a more positive experience?

Reframing your mindset involves shifting from a focus on limitations to a focus on possibilities, embracing the opportunities for learning, adventure, and connection that come with aging and retirement.

5. What are some practical steps individuals can take to prepare for and embrace "Their Final Third" of life?

Practical steps include assessing financial readiness for retirement, prioritizing physical and mental well-being, cultivating social connections, and exploring new interests and passions.

Reflection

Take a moment to reflect on the insights and lessons you've gained from this section.

Consider how you can apply this knowledge to your own life and plans for the future.

Use this space to jot down your thoughts, ideas, and action steps as you continue on your journey towards a fulfilling retirement.

Moving on...

As we've explored in this section, the importance of personal development, fitness, and financial planning cannot be overstated when preparing for the "Your Final Third".

Just as a strong foundation is essential for building a sturdy house, these foundational elements serve as the bedrock for a fulfilling retirement experience.

Now, as we turn our attention to the next section, we dive deeper into the practical strategies and considerations for optimizing your personal well-being in retirement.

From staying physically active and mentally sharp to the value of pursuing hobbies and passions, Section I offers invaluable insights and actionable advice to help you thrive in the golden years ahead.

So let us embark on this journey together, armed with the knowledge, tools, and motivation to embrace the challenges and opportunities that lie ahead.

With each step forward, may you find renewed energy, purpose, and enthusiasm for the adventure of retirement living.

"You're never too old to set another goal or to dream a new dream."

- C.S. Lewis

Section I: Personal Development & Fitness

This section emphasizes the importance of both physical and mental well-being in "Your Final Third", as well as the value of pursuing hobbies and passions for a fulfilling retirement.

Introduction to Personal Development & Fitness

In the journey of life, our well-being encompasses not only our financial security but also our physical and mental health. As we enter "the final third", nurturing our personal development and prioritizing fitness become essential pillars for embracing the richness and vitality of retirement.

Section I of "Your Final Third" is dedicated to exploring these critical aspects of retirement preparation, offering practical guidance and inspiration to help you cultivate a vibrant and fulfilling lifestyle in the years ahead.

From staying physically active and mentally agile to discovering new passions and pursuits, this section empowers you to invest in your well-being and unlock the full potential of your golden years.

As we embark on this journey together, let us recognize the profound impact that personal development and fitness have on our overall quality of life.

Beyond the pursuit of financial security, retirement presents us with a unique opportunity to focus on self-care, personal growth, and meaningful experiences that enrich our lives and nourish our souls.

Through the pages that follow, you'll find a wealth of insights, strategies, and practical tips to help you thrive in all aspects of your personal well-being.

Whether you're seeking to maintain an active lifestyle, sharpen your cognitive abilities, or explore new passions and hobbies, this section is your guide to unlocking the full potential of your physical, mental, and emotional health.

So let us embark on this journey with open hearts and curious minds, embracing the opportunity to invest in ourselves and cultivate a life of purpose, vitality, and fulfillment in the final third of our journey.

Together, let us discover the transformative power of personal development and fitness as we embark on the adventure of retirement living.

Staying Active, Staying Vibrant

Physical activity is not just for the young; it's essential for maintaining vitality and well-being at any age. In this sub-section, we'll explore the importance of staying active as you enter "Your Final Third".

From daily walks to yoga to strength training, there are countless ways to incorporate movement into your routine and reap the benefits of improved health and longevity.

We'll also discuss how staying active can help prevent common age-related ailments such as heart disease, diabetes, and arthritis, allowing you to enjoy a higher quality of life well into your golden years.

Cardiovascular Health

Regular exercise, particularly aerobic activities such as walking, swimming, or cycling, helps strengthen the heart and improve circulation, reducing the risk of heart disease and stroke.

Exercise helps lower blood pressure, cholesterol levels, and triglycerides, which are all risk factors for cardiovascular disease.

By maintaining a healthy weight and promoting efficient blood flow, regular physical activity supports overall heart health and reduces the likelihood of developing heart-related issues as you age.

Diabetes Prevention and Management

Physical activity plays a crucial role in preventing Type 2 diabetes by improving insulin sensitivity and blood sugar control.

Exercise helps lower blood glucose levels and reduce the risk of insulin resistance, a key factor in the development of Type 2 diabetes.

For those already living with diabetes, regular physical activity can help manage blood sugar levels, reduce the need for medication, and lower the risk of complications such as nerve damage and cardiovascular disease.

Joint Health and Arthritis Management

Contrary to common belief, regular exercise can be beneficial for joint health and arthritis management.

Low-impact activities such as walking, swimming, and yoga help strengthen the muscles around the joints, improve flexibility, and reduce stiffness and pain.

Exercise helps lubricate the joints and promote  cartilage health, which can alleviate symptoms of arthritis and delay the progression of degenerative joint diseases.

By maintaining an active lifestyle, you can preserve mobility and independence, allowing you to continue enjoying your favorite activities well into your golden years.

Mental Health and Well-being

In addition to its physical benefits, regular physical activity also has positive effects on mental health and well-being.

Exercise releases endorphins, neurotransmitters that promote feelings of happiness and reduce stress and anxiety.

Staying active can help improve sleep quality, boost cognitive function, and enhance overall mood and self-esteem, contributing to a higher quality of life as you age.

In conclusion, staying active is essential for promoting physical health, preventing common age-related ailments, and enhancing overall well-being in your golden years.

By incorporating regular exercise into your daily routine, you can enjoy a higher quality of life, maintain independence, and continue pursuing the activities you love well into your later years.

Mental Agility: Keeping Your Mind Sharp

Just as physical exercise is vital for maintaining a healthy body, mental stimulation is crucial for preserving cognitive function and mental acuity as you age.

In this sub-section, we'll explore various strategies and activities to keep your mind sharp and engaged. From puzzles and brain games to lifelong learning and social interaction, there are numerous ways to challenge your brain and foster neuroplasticity.

We'll also discuss the importance of maintaining a positive mindset and how cultivating resilience can help you navigate the inevitable challenges that come with aging.

Maintaining a positive mindset and cultivating resilience are essential components of aging gracefully and navigating the inevitable challenges that come with growing older. Here's why:

Psychological Well-being

A positive mindset can significantly impact your psychological well-being, helping you maintain a sense of optimism, purpose, and satisfaction with life as you age.

Cultivating a resilient outlook allows you to approach challenges with resilience, adaptability, and a growth mindset, enabling you to bounce back from setbacks and persevere in the face of adversity.

Physical Health

Research has shown that individuals with a positive outlook on aging tend to have better physical health outcomes and a lower risk of chronic diseases and disabilities.

Maintaining a positive mindset can reduce stress levels, lower inflammation in the body, and strengthen the immune system, all of which contribute to better overall health and longevity.

Coping with Change

Aging inevitably brings changes, such as physical decline, loss of loved ones, and transitions in roles and responsibilities.

Cultivating resilience allows you to adapt to these changes with grace and acceptance, rather than resistance or despair.

By embracing change as a natural part of life and focusing on what you can control, you can navigate transitions more effectively and find new sources of meaning and fulfillment in your later years.

Social Connection and Support

Maintaining a positive mindset can enhance your social connections and support networks, which are crucial for emotional well-being and resilience.

Positive individuals tend to attract others with their uplifting energy and outlook, fostering deeper connections and a sense of belonging within their communities.

Social support plays a critical role in helping individuals cope with stress, overcome challenges, and find comfort and solace during difficult times.

Enhanced Problem-Solving Skills

Cultivating resilience involves developing problem-solving skills, emotional intelligence, and coping strategies that enable you to navigate life's ups and downs with grace and poise.

Resilient individuals are better equipped to identify solutions, seek support when needed, and persevere in the face of adversity, ultimately leading to greater personal growth and self-confidence.

Reading

With more leisure time in your later years, it is a wonderful opportunity to embrace reading for both personal development and pleasure. Engaging with books can provide significant cognitive benefits, such as keeping the brain active and improving memory function.

This mental stimulation helps to maintain critical thinking skills and can slow cognitive decline, contributing to overall brain health. Moreover, reading can serve as a stress reliever, offering an escape from daily worries and fostering emotional well-being. The joy of finishing a book can also boost self-esteem and provide a sense of accomplishment.

Additionally, reading enables lifelong learning and personal growth. It allows you to explore new interests, stay informed about the world, and develop a broader cultural awareness.

Socially, joining book clubs or discussion groups can create a sense of community and provide valuable social interactions. Practical considerations, such as access to large print books, audiobooks, and e-readers, ensure that you can enjoy reading regardless of physical limitations.

Ultimately, the pleasure and entertainment derived from exploring diverse genres and narratives can enrich your life, offering you endless adventures and insights without even leaving the comfort of your home.

In conclusion, maintaining a positive mindset and cultivating resilience are essential for navigating the inevitable challenges that come with aging.

By fostering optimism, adaptability, and a growth mindset, you can enhance your psychological well-being, cope more effectively with change, and embrace the later years of life with grace and resilience.

Embracing New Hobbies and Passions

Retirement offers the perfect opportunity to explore new interests and passions that may have been put on hold during your working years.

Whether it's painting, gardening, photography, or learning a new language, embracing hobbies can bring joy, fulfillment, and a sense of purpose to your life.

In this sub-section, we'll discuss the benefits of pursuing hobbies in "Your Final Third", including reduced stress, enhanced creativity, and improved overall well-being.

We'll also provide practical tips for discovering new interests and integrating them into your daily routine.

Staying active is crucial for maintaining physical health and preventing common age-related ailments such as heart disease, diabetes, and arthritis.

Let's dive deeper into how regular physical activity can help promote a higher quality of life well into your golden years:

Pursuing hobbies in "Your Final Third" offers numerous benefits for overall well-being, including reduced stress, enhanced creativity, and improved mental and physical health. Let's explore these benefits in more detail and provide practical tips for discovering new interests and integrating them into your daily routine:

Reduced Stress and Anxiety

Engaging in hobbies provides a healthy outlet for stress and anxiety, allowing you to unwind and relax after a busy day.

Immersing yourself in activities you enjoy can help distract your mind from worries and negative thoughts, promoting a sense of calm and tranquility.

Enhanced Creativity and Cognitive Function

Hobbies stimulate the brain and encourage creative thinking, helping to keep the mind sharp and agile as you age.

Exploring new interests and learning new skills challenges the brain, fostering neural connections and promoting cognitive health.

Improved Overall Well-being

Pursuing hobbies that bring you joy and fulfillment contributes to a greater sense of overall well-being and life satisfaction.

Hobbies provide a sense of purpose and accomplishment, boosting self-esteem and confidence in your abilities.

Social Connection and Community

Many hobbies offer opportunities for social interaction and connection with like-minded individuals, fostering friendships and a sense of belonging.

Joining clubs, groups, or classes related to your hobbies can provide a supportive community where you can share experiences, learn from others, and cultivate meaningful relationships.

Physical Health Benefits

Some hobbies, such as gardening, hiking, or dancing, offer physical activity and exercise, which are essential for maintaining health and mobility as you age.

Engaging in regular physical activity through hobbies can improve cardiovascular health, strengthen muscles and bones, and reduce the risk of chronic diseases.

Practical Tips for Discovering and Pursuing Hobbies:

1. Explore Your Interests:

Reflect on activities you enjoyed in the past or hobbies you've always wanted to try. Experiment with different activities to discover what brings you joy and fulfillment.

2. Start Small:

Don't feel pressured to master a new hobby right away. Start with small, manageable steps and gradually build your skills and confidence over time.

3. Set Realistic Goals:

Set achievable goals for your hobbies, whether it's completing a craft project, learning a new recipe, or exploring a new hiking trail. Celebrate your progress and accomplishments along the way.

4. Make Time for Your Hobbies:

Schedule regular time in your calendar for your hobbies, treating them as important appointments for self-care and personal growth.

5. Stay Flexible and Open-Minded:

Be open to trying new activities and exploring different interests. You may discover hidden talents or passions you never knew you had.

6. Connect with Others:

Seek out opportunities to connect with others who share your interests, whether it's joining a local club or attending workshops and events related to your hobbies.

By incorporating hobbies into your daily routine, you can enhance your overall well-being, reduce stress, and foster a greater sense of fulfillment and joy in your final third of life.

Whether it's painting, gardening, cooking, or playing music, finding activities that bring you happiness and satisfaction is essential for living a vibrant and fulfilling life at any age.

Reflection and Review

1. What are some strategies for staying physically active and mentally engaged in retirement?

Some strategies include regular exercise, engaging in hobbies and intellectual pursuits, and maintaining social connections.

2. How can mindfulness and meditation contribute to overall well-being in retirement?

Mindfulness and meditation can reduce stress, improve focus and concentration, and enhance emotional resilience.

3. Why is it important to explore new hobbies and passions in retirement?

Exploring new hobbies can provide a sense of purpose, fulfillment, and enjoyment, as well as stimulate creativity and cognitive function.

4. What are some practical tips for maintaining a healthy lifestyle as you age?

Tips include eating a balanced diet, getting regular exercise, staying socially connected, managing stress, and getting enough sleep.

5. How can regular physical activity help prevent age-related health conditions?

Regular physical activity can reduce the risk of chronic diseases such as heart disease, diabetes, and osteoporosis, as well as improve overall physical function and mobility.

Reflection

Take a moment to reflect on the insights and lessons you've gained from this section.

Consider how you can apply this knowledge to your own life and plans for the future.

Use this space to jot down your thoughts, ideas, and action steps as you continue on your journey towards a fulfilling retirement.

Moving on...

As we've explored the importance of nurturing our physical and mental well-being in the pursuit of a fulfilling retirement, we now shift our focus to another cornerstone of retirement readiness: financial planning.

Just as physical fitness is essential for maintaining our health and vitality, financial fitness is crucial for ensuring our long-term security and peace of mind.

In the sections preceding this transition, we've examined strategies for staying active, sharpening our minds, and embracing new passions and hobbies...all vital components of a vibrant retirement lifestyle.

Now, as we dive into the realm of financial planning, we recognize the interconnectedness of these aspects of well-being. A solid financial plan provides the foundation upon which we can build our retirement dreams, enabling us to pursue our passions, support our loved ones, and enjoy the fruits of our labor with confidence and security.

In the following section, we'll explore the intricacies of retirement savings, budgeting, investing, and more, offering insights, strategies, and practical advice to help you navigate the complexities of financial planning in retirement.

From understanding your retirement accounts and creating a sustainable budget to maximizing Social Security benefits and planning for healthcare costs, this section will empower you to make informed decisions and chart a course toward a prosperous and fulfilling retirement future.

So let us embark on this next phase of our journey together, armed with the knowledge and tools to achieve financial security and peace of mind in the golden years ahead.

By integrating the principles of personal development and fitness with sound financial planning, we can create a retirement lifestyle that nourishes both body and soul, enabling us to thrive in every aspect of our lives.

"The best time to plant a tree was 20 years ago. The second-best time is now."

- Chinese Proverb

Section II: Financial Planning

This section emphasizes the importance of financial preparedness and provides practical advice for managing retirement savings, creating a budget, and investing wisely in "Your Final Third".

Understanding Your Retirement Savings

As you enter "Your Final Third", having a clear understanding of your retirement savings is paramount.

In this sub-section, we'll dive into the various types of retirement accounts, such as 401(k)s, IRAs, and pensions, and discuss how to assess your current financial situation.

We'll explore strategies for maximizing your retirement savings, including catch-up contributions for those nearing retirement age and the importance of diversification to mitigate risk.

By gaining a comprehensive understanding of your retirement savings, you can make informed decisions and ensure a more secure financial future.

Let's dive into the various types of retirement accounts, including 401(k)s, IRAs, and pensions, as well as how to assess your current financial situation and strategies for maximizing your retirement savings:

Types of Retirement Accounts

401(k):

A 401(k) is an employer-sponsored retirement savings plan that allows employees to contribute a portion of their pre-tax income to a retirement account.

Employers may offer matching contributions up to a certain percentage of the employee's salary. Contributions to a traditional 401(k) are made on a pre-tax basis, meaning they reduce taxable income in the year of contribution, and withdrawals are taxed as ordinary income in retirement.

Some employers may also offer Roth 401(k) options, where contributions are made with after-tax dollars, but withdrawals in retirement are tax-free.

Individual Retirement Account (IRA):

An IRA is a tax-advantaged retirement savings account that individuals can open on their own, regardless of whether they have access to an employer-sponsored plan.

There are two main types of IRAs: Traditional and Roth.

Contributions to a Traditional IRA may be tax-deductible, depending on income level and whether the individual or their spouse has access to an employer-sponsored retirement plan.

Withdrawals from a traditional IRA are taxed as ordinary income in retirement.

In contrast, contributions to a Roth IRA are made with after-tax dollars, but qualified withdrawals in retirement are tax-free.

Pensions:

A pension is a retirement plan provided by an employer that promises a specific monthly benefit to employees upon retirement.

Pensions are funded by employer contributions and typically provide a guaranteed income stream for life to retirees.

However, pensions are less common in the private sector than they once were, with many employers transitioning to defined-contribution plans like 401(k)s.

It is important to note that distributions from 401(k) plans, Traditional IRAs, and Pensions can all affect the provisional income calculation, which is used to determine the tax treatment of Social Security benefits and potentially result in higher taxes on Social Security benefits.

We will discuss this further in the next section but It's important for retirees to be aware of the impact of retirement account distributions on their overall income and tax liability, including the potential taxation of Social Security benefits. Strategic planning, such as managing the timing and size of distributions, can help minimize tax implications and optimize retirement income.

Roths, LIRPs and Indexed Annuities; Tax Enhanced Alternatives

In considering whether a 401(k) or Traditional IRA is a wise choice as a retirement account, it's essential to weigh the potential for future tax increases against current tax benefits and investment options.

The following sub-section provides information on three key alternatives which may assist you to provide tax-free income during "Your Final Third". I purposely expanded this sub-section to provide more detailed information as I consider these alternatives often overlooked and/or misunderstood.

If you anticipate higher taxes in retirement, a Roth 401(k) or Roth IRA may also be worth considering, as qualified withdrawals from these accounts are tax-free, regardless of future tax rates. Additionally, diversifying retirement savings across multiple account types (e.g.,

Traditional IRA, Roth IRA, taxable accounts) can provide flexibility and tax advantages in retirement.

Consulting with a financial advisor or tax professional can help you evaluate your options and make informed decisions based on your individual circumstances and goals.

A Roth IRA conversion is the process of transferring funds from a Traditional IRA, 401(k), or other pre-tax retirement account into a Roth IRA. Unlike Traditional IRAs, contributions to Roth IRAs are made with after-tax dollars, but qualified withdrawals in retirement are tax-free.

Since Roth IRA distributions are tax-free and not included in your Adjusted Gross Income (AGI), they do not affect the taxation of Social Security benefits. Additionally, because Roth IRA distributions are not included in AGI, they do not impact Medicare premiums, which are based on income thresholds known as IRMAA, or Income-Related Monthly Adjustment Amount.

Benefits of Roth IRA Conversions

Tax Diversification: Converting funds to a Roth IRA can provide tax diversification in retirement by creating a source of tax-free income alongside taxable retirement accounts.

Tax-Free Growth: Once funds are in a Roth IRA, any earnings and growth within the account can grow tax-free, providing potential for greater accumulation over time.

No Required Minimum Distributions (RMDs): Roth IRAs are not subject to RMDs during the account owner's lifetime, allowing for greater flexibility in retirement income planning and potentially reducing tax obligations in later years.

Estate Planning Benefits: Roth IRAs offer favorable estate planning advantages, as heirs can inherit Roth IRAs tax-free and enjoy tax-free withdrawals, subject to certain requirements.

Considerations Before Converting

Tax Implications: Converting funds to a Roth IRA requires paying income taxes on the amount converted in the year of the conversion. Individuals should consider their current and future tax brackets to assess the impact on their tax liability.

Ability to Pay Taxes: Taxpayers should have sufficient funds outside of the retirement account to pay the taxes owed on the conversion without dipping into retirement savings.

Time Horizon: Roth IRA conversions are most beneficial for individuals with a longer time horizon before retirement, as there is more time for tax-free growth to offset the upfront tax cost of the conversion.

Strategies for Roth IRA Conversions

Partial Conversions: Rather than converting the entire balance at once, individuals can consider partial conversions over several years to manage tax liabilities and spread out the tax burden.

Timing: Conversions may be strategically timed during years with lower income or tax rates, such as during early retirement or before reaching the age when your Required Minimum Distributions (RMD) begin.

Recharacterization: In certain situations, individuals may have the option to undo or "recharacterize" a Roth IRA conversion if circumstances change or if the conversion results in unintended tax consequences.

Roth IRA conversions can be a powerful tool for managing tax exposure in retirement and enhancing long-term financial flexibility. By understanding the benefits, considerations, and strategies involved, individuals can make informed decisions about whether Roth IRA conversions are appropriate for their retirement planning needs.

<u>A Life Insurance Retirement Plan (LIRP)</u>, also known as an Indexed Universal Life (IUL) insurance policy, is a type of permanent life insurance that offers a death benefit along with a cash value component that can accumulate over time.

Unlike term life insurance, which provides coverage for a specific period, permanent life insurance provides coverage for the insured's entire life as long as premiums are paid.

Tax Advantages:

LIRPs offer **tax-deferred growth** on the cash value component, meaning that policyholders can accumulate funds within the policy without paying taxes on the growth.

Policyholders can access the cash value of the LIRP through tax-free withdrawals or loans, allowing them to supplement retirement income without triggering taxable income.

Flexibility and Control:

LIRPs offer flexibility in premium payments, allowing policyholders to adjust the amount and frequency of their contributions based on their financial circumstances.

Policyholders have control over how they allocate their cash value among different investment options, which may include indexed accounts tied to stock market performance.

Guarantees and Protections:

LIRPs typically offer various guarantees, such as a guaranteed minimum interest rate on the cash value, to protect against market downturns and ensure steady growth.

Some LIRPs offer optional riders or features, such as living benefits riders, that provide additional protection against disability, chronic illness, or long-term care needs.

A long-term care rider on a LIRP provides coverage for qualified long-term care expenses, such as nursing home care, assisted living facilities, in-home care, and other LTC services.

If the policyholder requires long-term care, they can access a portion of the death benefit or cash value of the LIRP to help cover the cost of care, subject to the terms and conditions of the rider.

Any LTC benefits paid out are typically deducted from the policy's death benefit, which can affect the amount received by beneficiaries.

Estate Planning Benefits:

The death benefit of a LIRP can provide financial security for beneficiaries and may be paid out tax-free, providing a source of liquidity to cover estate taxes or other expenses.

LIRPs can be used as part of an estate planning strategy to transfer wealth to heirs in a tax-efficient manner, especially for individuals with large estates subject to estate taxes.

Considerations and Risks:

While LIRPs offer tax advantages and potential for cash value growth, they may also come with higher fees and costs compared to other investment options.

Policyholders should carefully consider factors such as premium payments, surrender charges, and policy illustrations to ensure that a LIRP aligns with their financial goals and risk tolerance.

It's essential to review the terms and features of the LIRP policy, including any limitations or restrictions on withdrawals, to understand how the policy works and its potential impact on retirement planning.

Indexed Annuities are insurance products designed to provide retirement income and potential growth opportunities linked to the performance of a specified stock market index, such as the S&P 500.

Indexed annuities offer both principal protection and the potential for higher returns compared to traditional fixed annuities, making them a popular choice for retirees seeking growth potential with limited downside risk.

Tax-Deferred Growth:

One of the primary tax advantages of indexed annuities is tax-deferred growth on the accumulated value within the annuity. This means that earnings within the annuity grow tax-free until withdrawn, allowing for potentially greater accumulation over time.

Index-Linked Returns:

Indexed annuities offer returns linked to the performance of a stock market index, typically through participation rates, caps, or spreads. When the index performs well, annuity holders may receive credited interest based on a portion of the index's gains, subject to limitations.

Principal Protection:

Indexed annuities typically come with a minimum guaranteed interest rate, ensuring that the annuity's principal value is protected from market downturns. This feature provides retirees with peace of mind knowing that their investment is shielded from loss.

Income Options:

Indexed annuities offer various income options, including lifetime income streams, fixed-period payments, or lump-sum withdrawals. Retirees can choose a payout option that suits their retirement income needs and preferences, providing a steady stream of income throughout retirement.

Riders and Features:

Indexed annuities may offer optional riders or features, such as guaranteed minimum withdrawal benefits (GMWBs) or enhanced death benefits, that provide additional protection, or income guarantees for retirees and their beneficiaries.

Considerations and Risks:

While indexed annuities offer potential for growth and downside protection, they may also come with limitations, such as participation rates, caps, or surrender charges.

Retirees should carefully review the terms and features of indexed annuities, including fees, charges, and contract provisions, to ensure they understand how the annuity works and its potential impact on retirement planning.

Regarding Roths, LIRPs and Indexed Annuities, as  *discussed previously, it's always advisable to consult with a financial advisor or tax professional for personalized guidance based on your individual circumstances.*

Assessing Your Current Financial Situation

1. Start by taking stock of your current assets, including savings, investments, and retirement accounts, as well as any debts or liabilities.

2. Evaluate your current income, expenses, and cash flow to determine how much you can afford to save for retirement each month.

3. Consider factors such as your age, desired retirement age, life expectancy, and expected retirement lifestyle when assessing your retirement needs and goals.

4. Take into account any employer-sponsored retirement benefits, such as 401(k) matching contributions or pension benefits, when calculating your retirement savings target.

5. One online source that may be useful to you is boldin.com, formerly newretirement.com. You will find free resources such as planning tools and calculators.

Strategies for Maximizing Retirement Savings

1. Take advantage of employer-sponsored retirement plans like 401(k)s, especially if your employer offers matching contributions. Contribute enough to maximize the employer match, as this is essentially free money that boosts your retirement savings.

2. Consider contributing to an IRA, either traditional or Roth, to supplement your employer-sponsored retirement savings. Even if you have access to a 401(k), an IRA can provide additional tax-advantaged savings opportunities.

3. Automate your savings by setting up automatic contributions to your retirement accounts each month. This helps ensure consistent savings and reduces the temptation to spend money earmarked for retirement.

4. Review and adjust your investment portfolio regularly to ensure it aligns with your risk tolerance, time horizon, and retirement goals. Consider diversifying your investments across different asset classes to mitigate risk and maximize returns over the long term.

5. Take advantage of catch-up contributions if you're age 50 or older. Both 401(k)s and IRAs allow for additional catch-up contributions beyond the standard contribution limits for older individuals.

6. Consider seeking advice from a financial advisor or retirement planner to develop a personalized retirement savings strategy tailored to your individual circumstances and goals.

By understanding the various types of retirement accounts available, assessing your current financial situation, and implementing strategies to maximize your retirement savings, you can take proactive steps to secure a comfortable and financially secure retirement.

Creating a Sustainable Budget

Budgeting is a cornerstone of financial planning at any age, but it takes on added importance as you transition into retirement.

In this sub-section, we'll discuss the importance of creating a sustainable budget that aligns with your lifestyle and retirement goals.

We'll explore strategies for estimating your expenses in retirement, including healthcare costs, housing, and leisure activities, and provide practical tips for managing your finances effectively.

From tracking your spending to exploring ways to reduce expenses, we'll help you develop a budget that allows you to live comfortably while maintaining financial stability.

Creating a sustainable budget that aligns with your lifestyle and retirement goals is essential for achieving financial stability and peace of mind in retirement.

Here's why it's important, along with strategies for estimating your expenses and practical tips for managing your finances effectively...

Importance of Creating a Sustainable Budget

A budget serves as a roadmap for your financial future, helping you allocate resources wisely and prioritize spending based on your values and goals.

In retirement, having a sustainable budget ensures that you can cover essential expenses such as housing, healthcare, and daily living costs without depleting your savings too quickly.

By living within your means and adhering to a budget, you can minimize financial stress and uncertainty, allowing you to enjoy your retirement years with confidence and peace of mind.

Estimating Expenses in Retirement

Start by assessing your current spending habits and lifestyle to get a baseline understanding of your expenses.

Consider factors such as:

1. Housing costs (including mortgage or rent, property taxes, and maintenance)

2. Healthcare expenses (including insurance premiums, out-of-pocket costs, and long-term care), and,

3. Leisure activities (such as travel, dining out, and entertainment)

Don't forget to account for inflation and potential increases in expenses over time, especially for healthcare costs, which tend to rise as individuals age.

Practical Tips for Managing Finances Effectively

Track your spending: Use budgeting tools or apps to monitor your expenses and identify areas where you may be overspending or could cut back.

Prioritize essential expenses: Allocate a portion of your budget to cover essential needs such as housing, healthcare, and food before allocating funds to discretionary expenses.

Build an emergency fund: Set aside funds (typically six months of living expenses) in a separate savings account to cover unexpected expenses or emergencies, such as medical bills or home repairs, without having to dip into your retirement savings.

Review and adjust your budget regularly: Periodically review your budget to ensure it remains aligned with your current financial situation and retirement goals. Adjust as needed to accommodate changes in income, expenses, or priorities.

Exploring Ways to Reduce Expenses

Identify areas where you can cut back on non-essential spending, such as dining out, subscription services, or impulse purchases.

Look for opportunities to save on recurring expenses, such as renegotiating bills for services like cable, internet, or insurance, or shopping around for better deals on utilities or healthcare plans.

Consider downsizing or rightsizing your living arrangements to reduce housing costs and free up funds for other priorities.

Take advantage of discounts, coupons, and loyalty programs to save money on everyday purchases and activities.

Developing a Budget for Comfortable Living and Financial Stability

Aim to strike a balance between enjoying your retirement and maintaining financial stability by prioritizing spending on experiences and activities that bring you joy and fulfillment while being mindful of your long-term financial goals.

Allocate funds for both current needs and future goals, such as travel, hobbies, and healthcare, as well as savings for emergencies, major purchases, and retirement income.

Be realistic about your income and expenses and be willing to make adjustments as needed to stay on track with your budget and financial plan.

What about Reverse Mortgages?

I often get asked about Home Equity Conversion Mortgages (HECM) and Traditional Reverse Mortgages so here's a deep dive into these options as a tax-efficient strategy for accessing home equity in retirement.

A Home Equity Conversion Mortgage (HECM) and a Traditional Reverse Mortgage share similarities but also have some key differences. Here's an overview of each:

Traditional Reverse Mortgage:

A traditional reverse mortgage is a loan product available to homeowners aged 62 or older, allowing them to convert a portion of their home equity into cash.

The homeowner receives funds from the lender, either as a lump sum, monthly payments, a line of credit, or a combination of these options, without the need to make monthly mortgage payments.

The loan is repaid when the homeowner moves out of the home, sells the home, or passes away. At that time, the loan balance, along with any accrued interest and fees, is typically paid off using the proceeds from the sale of the home.

Traditional reverse mortgages are offered by private lenders and are not insured by the federal government.

Home Equity Conversion Mortgage (HECM):

A HECM is a type of reverse mortgage that is

insured by the Federal Housing Administration (FHA), a division of the U.S. Department of Housing and Urban Development (HUD).

HECMs offer the same basic features as traditional reverse mortgages, including allowing homeowners aged 62 or older to access their home equity without making monthly mortgage payments.

One key difference is that HECMs have certain borrower protections and requirements mandated by the FHA, such as financial counseling for borrowers, limits on loan fees, and restrictions on loan amounts.

HECMs also offer additional flexibility and features, such as the option to choose between fixed-rate and adjustable-rate loan options, as well as a feature called a "growth" or "credit line growth" feature, which allows the available line of credit to increase over time, providing potential for greater borrowing power in the future.

Another important distinction is that HECMs are subject to certain property eligibility requirements, such as the home must be the borrower's primary residence and meet FHA property standards.

A little more about HECM's:

Tax Implications:

HECM proceeds are typically considered loan advances rather than taxable income, so they are not subject to federal income tax.

Because HECM funds are borrowed against the equity in the home, they are not considered taxable income by the IRS. This means that homeowners can access their home equity without incurring a tax liability.

Flexibility and Control:

Borrowers retain ownership of their home and can continue to live in it as long as they meet the loan requirements, such as maintaining the property and paying property taxes and homeowners insurance.

HECM borrowers have flexibility in how they use the loan proceeds, whether for supplementing retirement income, covering healthcare expenses, making home renovations, or funding other expenses.

Repayment Options:

HECMs do not require monthly mortgage payments like traditional mortgages. Instead, the loan balance accrues over time, and repayment is typically deferred until the borrower sells the home, moves out permanently, or passes away.

When the loan becomes due, the borrower or their heirs can repay the loan balance by selling the home or using other assets. If the home is sold for more than the loan balance, the borrower or their heirs keep the remaining equity.

Safeguards and Protections:

HECMs are subject to strict regulations and consumer protections to safeguard borrowers' interests. These include mandatory counseling sessions to ensure borrowers understand the terms and implications of the loan, as well as limits on fees and charges.

The FHA insurance on HECMs protects borrowers and lenders by guaranteeing that borrowers will continue to receive payments even if the lender defaults.

Considerations and Risks:

While HECMs can be a valuable financial tool for retirees, they are not suitable for everyone. Borrowers should carefully consider factors such as interest rates, fees, loan terms, and their long-term housing and financial goals before deciding to pursue a HECM.

Potential risks associated with HECMs include the accumulation of interest over time, which can reduce the equity remaining in the home, and the possibility of foreclosure if borrowers fail to meet their loan obligations.

In summary, while both traditional reverse mortgages and HECMs provide homeowners with a way to access their home equity without making monthly mortgage payments, HECMs are specifically designed to meet certain FHA standards and offer additional borrower protections and features not found in traditional reverse mortgages.

By considering all of your options and creating a sustainable budget that aligns with your lifestyle and retirement goals, estimating expenses accurately, and implementing practical tips for managing your finances effectively, you can achieve financial stability and enjoy a comfortable retirement without sacrificing the things that matter most to you.

Investing in Your Future

Retirement is not the end of your financial journey; it's a new beginning.

In this sub-section, we'll explore the importance of continuing to invest in your future during "Your Final Third".

We'll discuss strategies for managing your investments in retirement, including asset allocation, risk tolerance, and the role of annuities and other income-generating vehicles.

We'll also address common concerns such as market volatility and inflation and provide guidance on adjusting your investment strategy as you age.

By taking a proactive approach to investing, you can ensure a steady stream of income and enjoy a more financially secure retirement.

Continuing to invest in your future during your final third of life is crucial for maintaining financial security, preserving purchasing power, and ensuring a comfortable retirement.

Here's why it's important, along with strategies for managing your investments, addressing common concerns, and adjusting your investment strategy as you age:

Importance of Continuing to Invest

Investing in retirement is essential for preserving and growing your wealth over time, especially as you no longer have a regular paycheck from employment.

By continuing to invest, you can generate additional income to supplement Social Security, pension benefits, and other sources of retirement income, helping to maintain your standard of living and cover expenses in retirement.

Investing also helps to hedge against inflation, which erodes the purchasing power of your savings over time. By earning a return on your investments that outpaces inflation, you can ensure that your money retains its value and can support your lifestyle throughout retirement.

Strategies for Managing Investments in Retirement

Asset Allocation:

Determine an appropriate asset allocation strategy based on your risk tolerance, time horizon, and retirement goals.

Consider diversifying your investments across different asset classes, such as stocks, bonds, and real estate, to manage risk and optimize returns.

Risk Tolerance:

Assess your risk tolerance carefully and adjust your investment portfolio accordingly.

As you approach retirement, you may want to gradually shift towards a more conservative investment approach to protect against market volatility and preserve capital.

Role of Annuities and Income-Generating Vehicles:

Consider incorporating annuities and other income-generating vehicles into your retirement portfolio to provide a steady stream of income in retirement.

Annuities can offer guaranteed income for life, protection against longevity risk, and peace of mind in retirement.

Addressing Common Concerns

Market Volatility:

Market volatility is a common concern for retirees, as it can impact the value of their investment portfolio and potentially erode savings.

To mitigate the impact of market volatility, maintain a diversified portfolio, stay focused on long-term goals, and avoid making knee-jerk reactions to short-term market fluctuations.

Inflation:

Inflation erodes the purchasing power of your savings over time, reducing the real value of your retirement income.

To combat inflation, invest in assets that have historically outpaced inflation, such as stocks and real estate, and consider incorporating inflation-protected securities into your portfolio, such as

Treasury Inflation-Protected Securities (TIPS).

Guidance on Adjusting Investment Strategy as You Age

As you age, consider gradually shifting towards a more conservative investment strategy to protect against market volatility and preserve capital.

This may involve reducing exposure to stocks and increasing allocation to bonds and other fixed-income investments.

Reassess your investment goals and risk tolerance periodically and make adjustments to your investment portfolio as needed.

As you move further into retirement, focus on generating a reliable stream of income to cover expenses and maintain financial stability.

In conclusion, continuing to invest in your future during your final third of life is essential for maintaining financial security, preserving purchasing power, and ensuring a comfortable retirement.

By implementing strategies for managing investments, addressing common concerns, and adjusting your investment strategy as you age, you can achieve your retirement goals and enjoy a financially secure and fulfilling retirement.

Reflection and Review

1. Why is it important to understand your retirement savings and investment options?

Understanding your options allows you to make informed decisions about saving for retirement, maximizing returns, and managing risk.

2. What are some key components of a sustainable budget in retirement?

Components include estimating expenses, managing debt, creating an emergency fund, and adjusting spending as needed.

3. How can diversification help protect your investment portfolio in retirement?

Diversification spreads investment risk across different asset classes, reducing exposure to market volatility and potential losses.

4. What factors should you consider when deciding when to claim Social Security benefits?

Factors include your full retirement age, financial needs, health status, and life expectancy.

5. Why is it important to plan for healthcare costs in retirement?

Healthcare costs can be significant in retirement, and planning ahead can help ensure you have adequate coverage and resources to meet your needs.

Reflection

Take a moment to reflect on the insights and lessons you've gained from this section.

Consider how you can apply this knowledge to your own life and plans for the future.

Use this space to jot down your thoughts, ideas, and action steps as you continue on your journey towards a fulfilling retirement.

Moving on...

Having laid the groundwork for financial security in retirement through careful planning and strategic decision-making, we now turn our attention to another crucial aspect of retirement preparedness: navigating the complexities of Social Security and Medicare.

As we've explored in the Financial Planning section, ensuring a sustainable budget, maximizing retirement savings, and making informed investment decisions are essential steps in securing your financial future.

However, understanding the intricacies of Social Security benefits and healthcare coverage through Medicare is equally vital for achieving comprehensive retirement readiness.

In the following section, we dive into the nuances of Social Security and Medicare, offering insights, strategies, and practical advice to help you make informed decisions about your retirement benefits and healthcare options.

From maximizing / optimizing Social Security benefits to deciphering the various parts of Medicare and planning for healthcare costs, this section provides invaluable guidance for navigating the maze of government programs and insurance policies in retirement.

So let us embark on this journey together, armed with the knowledge and confidence to navigate the complexities of Social Security and Medicare with clarity, competence, and peace of mind.

By understanding your rights, options, and responsibilities, you can make empowered decisions that enhance your financial security and well-being in the golden years ahead.

"Old age is an excellent time for outrage. My goal is to say or do at least one outrageous thing every week."

- Maggie Kuhn

Section III: Navigating Social Security & Medicare

This section addresses the complexities of Social Security and Medicare and provides practical guidance for maximizing benefits and planning for healthcare costs in "Your Final Third".

Before we discuss Social Security Strategy, I first want to address the most frequently asked question that I am asked on the subject, "How Reliable Will Social Security Be in the Future?"

Most Americans assume that Social Security will still be available at retirement. But will it?

Social Security was started in 1935 by President Roosevelt. The program at that time only supported retired workers. It now also includes benefits for spouses, minor children, and disabled workers.

At its inception, there were around 40 workers paying into the system for each retiree. Now the ratio is more like 3 to 1 and it will sink even lower. More money is removed from the program each year, and currently, the Social Security program is paying out more money than it's taking in.

In our personal lives, less money coming in and more money going out usually leads to bankruptcy. Unlike us, the government simply changes the rules, and changes indeed are necessary to keep the Social Security Program solvent.

We've been cautioned about the long-term solvency of Social Security for at least 40 years. Life expectancies continue to increase, and the number of seniors has never been greater plus there will also be a lower percentage of workers in the future.

From 1983 until 2010, the Social Security Program was running a surplus. That excess money was placed in a trust fund. Normally, the Social Security payments are made to retirees using Social Security taxes from current workers.

Social Security is beginning to dip into that excess due to a short fall. More money is being paid in benefits than the government is collecting in Social Security taxes. It's believed that the excess money will run out in 2034.

If nothing changes, at that point, the current workers will only be able to cover around 80% of the necessary payments.

The current law doesn't permit greater payments than the amount supported by Social Security taxes and the surplus. Congress could intervene and change the law. It's also possible that Social Security taxes could be raised.

Current proposals seek to raise the retirement age even higher, pay less in benefits, or increase taxes. The issue is a political hot potato, and I strongly suggest that you write a letter of concern to your Representatives and Senators.

This just highlights the importance of retirement planning. With proper saving and investing habits, Social Security could be just the icing on the cake.

Despite the fact that you may have paid into the system for many years, it would be a wise move to rely more on yourself, and less on the government, for most of your retirement funds.

Maximizing Social Security Benefits

Regardless of the current state of the Social Security Program, the reality is that Social Security serves as a crucial source of income for many retirees, and navigating its complexities can be daunting.

In this sub-section, we'll discuss strategies for maximizing your Social Security benefits to ensure a more financially secure retirement.

 We'll explore factors such as your retirement age, earnings history, and spousal benefits, and provide guidance on when and how to claim Social Security to maximize your lifetime benefits.

Whether you're approaching retirement or already receiving Social Security, understanding your options can make a significant difference in your financial well-being in "Your Final Third".

| Age to Receive Full Social Security Benefits ||
Year of Birth	Full Retirement Age
1937 or earlier	65
1938	65 and 2 months
1939	65 and 4 months
1940	65 and 6 months
1941	65 and 8 months
1942	65 and 10 months
1943-1954	66
1955	66 and 2 months
1956	66 and 4 months
1957	66 and 6 months
1958	66 and 8 months
1959	66 and 10 months
1960 and later	67
	Source: SSA.gov

Maximizing/Optimizing your Social Security benefits is crucial for ensuring a more financially secure retirement.

Here are strategies to consider, taking into account factors such as retirement age, earnings history, spousal benefits, and guidance on when and how to claim Social Security to maximize your lifetime benefits:

1. Understand Your Full Retirement Age (FRA)

Your Full Retirement Age (FRA) is the age at which you can claim your full Social Security retirement benefit, based on your birth year. For most people, FRA falls between 66 and 67 years old.

Claiming benefits before your FRA results in a reduction in monthly benefits, while delaying benefits beyond your FRA can result in an increase in benefits up to age 70.

2. Review Your Earnings History

Your Social Security benefits are based on your highest 35 years of earnings, adjusted for inflation.

Review your earnings history to ensure that all earnings are accurately recorded. Your Social Security Statement is available to view online by opening a "*my* Social Security" account; go to ssa.gov to sign up.

It is important for people of all ages to learn about their future Social Security benefits and to review their current earnings history.

Consider working additional years if you have fewer than 35 years of substantial earnings, as each additional year of earnings may replace a year of lower earnings, potentially increasing your benefit amount.

3. Consider Spousal / Divorced Benefits

If you are married, you may be eligible for spousal benefits based on your spouse's earnings history, even if you have little or no earnings history of your own.

Spousal benefits can be worth up to 50% of your spouse's full retirement benefit, depending on your FRA and your spouse's claiming strategy.

If you're divorced, male or female, you may still be eligible to receive benefits based on your ex-spouse's earnings record.

To qualify...your marriage must have lasted at least 10 years, you and your ex are both at least 62 years old, and you must be currently single.

Additionally, if divorced less than 2 years, your ex-spouse must be collecting a retirement benefit. If divorced for over two years, you are both considered independently entitled and your ex-spouse does not have to be receiving their retirement benefit.

Similar to spousal benefits, you can receive up to 50% of your ex-spouse's full retirement age amount, and your claim will not affect the benefits your ex-spouse or their current spouse can receive.

4. Maximize Survivor Benefits

If you are the higher-earning spouse, delaying your Social Security benefits can maximize survivor benefits for your spouse in the event of your death.

Survivor benefits are based on the higher-earning spouse's benefit amount, so delaying benefits can result in a higher survivor benefit for your spouse.

5. Coordinate Benefits with Your Spouse

Coordinate your claiming strategy with your spouse to maximize your combined Social Security benefits.

Consider factors such as age difference, earnings history, health status, and retirement goals when determining the optimal claiming strategy for you and your spouse.

6. Consider Claiming Strategies

Delaying benefits beyond your FRA can result in a higher monthly benefit, up to age 70.

For each year you delay benefits beyond your FRA, your benefit increases by a certain percentage (currently 8%), known as Delayed Retirement Credits.

Alternatively, claiming benefits early (as early as age 62) results in a reduced monthly benefit but provides income sooner.

This may be beneficial if you have an immediate need for income or if you have a shorter life expectancy.

If you're eligible for benefits and decide to delay your claim, you might be able to receive six-month's worth of retroactive payments.

This means you can receive a lump sum payment covering the benefits you would have received during those months.

To qualify for retroactive benefits, you must be past your full retirement age.

Keep in mind that when you claim retroactive benefits, the Social Security Administration will consider your filing date as if you claimed benefits six months earlier. This means your monthly benefit amount will be slightly lower than if you had delayed without claiming retroactively.

Claiming retroactive benefits can be beneficial if you need a lump sum of money immediately, but it's important to understand how this decision affects your ongoing monthly benefits.

7. Taxation of Social Security Benefits

Yes, **up to 85% of your benefits may be taxable**. This usually happens if you have other "substantial" income (aka "provisional" income} in addition to your benefits.

Provisional income is calculated by adding up **three types of income**:

Adjusted Gross Income (AGI): This includes all taxable income, such as wages, interest, dividends, and retirement account distributions, including those from 401(k) plans, Traditional IRAs, and pensions.

Tax-Exempt Interest: This includes interest from municipal bonds or other tax-exempt investments.

One-Half of Social Security Benefits: Half of the annual Social Security benefits received by the taxpayer (or the taxpayer and their spouse if filing jointly) is added to the provisional income calculation.

The total provisional income is used to determine the portion of Social Security benefits subject to taxation. Here's how it currently works:

For single filers with provisional income between $25,000 and $34,000 ($32,000 to $44,000 for joint filers), up to 50% of Social Security benefits may be subject to taxation.

For single filers with provisional income above $34,000 ($44,000 for joint filers), up to 85% of Social Security benefits may be subject to taxation.

8. Seek Professional Advice

I strongly advise consulting with a Registered Social Security Analyst, financial advisor or retirement planner who specializes in Social Security planning to help you navigate the complexities of the Social Security system and develop a personalized claiming strategy based on your unique financial situation and goals.

A **Registered Social Security Analyst (RSSA)** can provide you with a multi-page "Social Security Roadmap" including your Annual & Monthly Benefits, Claiming Options, Filing Sequences, Survivor Benefits, Lifetime Benefits, Longevity Comparisons, Benefit Options Breakdowns as well as Strategy, Planning and Filing Guidance.

For a more comprehensive review, feel free to reach out to *Senior Solutions Today* for assistance and/or guidance at www.seniorsolutionstoday.com

By understanding the factors that impact your Social Security benefits and implementing strategies to maximize your benefits, you can ensure a more financially secure retirement and make the most of this important source of retirement income.

Decoding Medicare: What You Need to Know

Medicare plays a vital role in providing healthcare coverage for millions of Americans aged 65 and older but understanding its intricacies can be overwhelming.

In this sub-section, we'll decode Medicare and provide a comprehensive overview of its various parts, including:

Part A (Hospital Insurance)

Part B (Medical Insurance)

Part C (Medicare Advantage), and

Part D (Prescription Drug Coverage)

We'll discuss eligibility requirements, enrollment periods, coverage options, and out-of-pocket costs, helping you make informed decisions about your healthcare coverage in retirement.

Decoding Medicare is essential for anyone approaching retirement age or already enrolled in Medicare.

Here's a basic overview of its various parts, including eligibility requirements, enrollment periods, coverage options, and out-of-pocket costs.

General Eligibility:

• Individuals who are age 65 or older, as well as under the age of 65 who

meet certain disabilities or other requirements

• Individuals who are under 65 and have received disability benefits for

at least 24 months may also qualify.

• Anyone with End Stage Renal Disease (ESRD), or Amyotrophic

Lateral Sclerosis (ALS) will automatically qualify.

1. Part A (Hospital Insurance)

Eligibility:

Most individuals age 65 or older who are eligible for Social Security benefits are automatically enrolled in Medicare Part A, regardless of whether they are currently receiving Social Security benefits.

- Part A is usually premium free if you or your spouse have worked for 40 quarters, and paid into FICA taxes for those 10 years

- If your spouse has passed, you must have been married for at least 10 years to claim premium free Part A under their work history

- You must also be a U.S. citizen; or a Legal U.S. resident for at least 5 continuous years

Coverage:

Medicare Part A provides coverage for inpatient hospital care, some skilled nursing facility care, hospice care, and home health services.

Enrollment:

Initial enrollment in Medicare Part A typically occurs automatically when you turn 65, but you can choose to delay enrollment if you or your spouse are still working and have group health coverage through an employer or union.

Out-of-Pocket Costs:

While most beneficiaries do not pay a premium for Part A coverage (if they or their spouse paid sufficient Medicare taxes while working), there are deductible, and coinsurance costs associated with certain services; these costs are generally updated annually.

2. Part B (Medical Insurance)

Eligibility:

Medicare Part B is available to individuals age 65 or older who are eligible for Medicare Part A. Enrollment in Part B is optional and requires payment of a monthly premium.

Coverage:

Medicare Part B provides coverage for medically necessary services and supplies, including doctor visits, outpatient care, preventive services, and durable medical equipment.

Enrollment:

Initial enrollment in Medicare Part B is typically automatic if you are receiving Social Security benefits when you turn 65.

If you are not receiving Social Security benefits, you must actively enroll in Part B during your Initial Enrollment Period (IEP) or during a Special Enrollment Period (SEP) if you have qualifying circumstances.

You can delay enrollment if covered through an employer with more than 20 employees, known as creditable coverage. When this coverage ends it is important to obtain Part B coverage before long-term late enrollment penalties are applied.

Out-of-Pocket Costs:

Beneficiaries pay a monthly premium for Part B coverage, as well as annual deductibles and coinsurance for covered services.

• Your State may pay this premium for you, if you qualify for the Medicare Savings Program based on your income & assets.

• Higher incomes will result in higher premiums due to IRMAA.

• Premiums can come out of your monthly SS Check, or paid on a

quarterly bill through direct billing.

3. Part C (Medicare Advantage)

Eligibility:

Medicare Part C, also known as Medicare Advantage, is available to individuals who are enrolled in both Medicare Part A and Part B and live in the service area of a Medicare Advantage plan.

Coverage:

Medicare Advantage plans are offered by private insurance companies approved by Medicare and provide all benefits covered under Part A and Part B, often including additional benefits such as prescription drug coverage, vision, dental, and hearing services.

Enrollment:

Medicare beneficiaries can enroll in a Medicare Advantage plan during their Initial Enrollment Period (IEP), Annual Enrollment Period (AEP), Open Enrollment Period (OEP) or during a Special Enrollment Period (SEP) if they have qualifying circumstances.

Out-of-Pocket Costs:

Medicare Advantage plans may have different cost-sharing requirements, including copayments, coinsurance, and deductibles, depending on the plan.

4. Part D (Prescription Drug Coverage)

Eligibility:

Medicare Part D is available to individuals who are enrolled in Medicare Part A or Part B and live in the service area of a Medicare Part D plan.

Coverage:

Medicare Part D plans provide coverage for prescription drugs, including both brand-name and generic medications, and are offered by private insurance companies approved by Medicare.

Enrollment:

Medicare beneficiaries can enroll in a Medicare Part D plan during their Initial Enrollment Period (IEP), Annual Enrollment Period (AEP), or during a Special Enrollment Period (SEP) if they have qualifying circumstances.

Out-of-Pocket Costs:

Medicare Part D plans have monthly premiums, annual deductibles, and copayments or coinsurance for covered medications.

The specific costs vary depending on the plan and the medications covered.

In conclusion, understanding the various parts of Medicare, including Part A (Hospital Insurance), Part B (Medical Insurance), Part C (Medicare Advantage), and Part D (Prescription Drug Coverage), is essential for navigating the Medicare system and making informed decisions about your healthcare coverage in retirement.

By familiarizing yourself with eligibility requirements, enrollment periods, coverage options, and out-of-pocket costs, you can ensure that you have the coverage you need to stay healthy and financially secure in your later years.

Planning for Healthcare Costs

Healthcare costs can pose a significant financial burden for retirees, but proper planning can help mitigate this risk.

In this sub-section, we'll explore strategies for planning and budgeting for healthcare expenses in "Your Final Third".

By taking proactive steps to plan for healthcare expenses, you can protect your financial security and enjoy peace of mind in your retirement years.

Planning and budgeting for healthcare expenses in "Your Final Third" is crucial for maintaining your health and financial well-being.

Here are strategies to consider, from estimating healthcare needs to exploring supplemental coverage options such as Medigap (Medicare Supplement) policies and long-term care insurance, along with practical tips for managing healthcare costs effectively:

1. Estimate Healthcare Needs

Review your current health status and medical history to assess potential healthcare needs in retirement, including anticipated medical treatments, prescription medications, and preventive care.

Consider factors such as chronic conditions, family medical history, and lifestyle habits when estimating healthcare needs for yourself and your spouse.

2. Understand Medicare Coverage

Familiarize yourself with the coverage provided by Medicare Parts A and B, including deductibles, copayments, and coinsurance for covered services.

Explore additional coverage options, such as Medicare Advantage (Part C) and Medicare Part D prescription drug plans, to fill gaps in Medicare coverage and provide comprehensive healthcare benefits.

3. Explore Supplemental Coverage Options

Consider purchasing a Medigap (Medicare Supplement) policy to help cover out-of-pocket costs not covered by Medicare, such as deductibles, coinsurance, and copayments.

Evaluate long-term care insurance as a way to protect against the potentially high costs of long-term care services, such as nursing home care, assisted living, and in-home care, which are not covered by Medicare.

For those concerned about the high premium cost and the "use it or lose it" factor of a traditional long-term care policy, as discussed in Section II, perhaps a LIRP (Life Insurance Retirement Plan) may be an option for long-term care peace of mind.

Also consider other supplemental coverages such as Cancer, Stroke, Heart Attack, Dental, Vison, Hearing and Short-Term Care as they may provide key protection and/or assist with out-of-pocket costs, especially if your family history includes any of these conditions or circumstances.

4. Compare Costs and Coverage

Research different Medigap plans, long-term care, and supplemental insurance policies to compare costs, coverage options, and benefits.

Consider factors such as premiums, deductibles, coverage limits, and provider networks when evaluating options.

Take into account your personal healthcare needs, budget, and risk tolerance when selecting supplemental coverage options that best fit your individual circumstances.

For a more comprehensive review, feel free to reach out to Senior Solutions Today for assistance and/or guidance, at:

www.seniorsolutionstoday.com

5. Budget for Healthcare Expenses

Estimate annual healthcare expenses based on projected medical costs, including premiums, deductibles, copayments, and coinsurance for Medicare and supplemental coverage.

Include costs for prescription medications, routine medical exams, preventive care, dental and vision services, and any other healthcare-related expenses in your budget.

Set aside funds in a dedicated healthcare savings account or budget category to cover anticipated healthcare costs and adjust your budget as needed to accommodate unexpected medical expenses.

6. Manage Healthcare Costs Effectively

Take advantage of preventive care services covered by Medicare, such as annual wellness exams, screenings, and immunizations, to maintain your health and detect potential health issues early.

Consider using generic medications and participating in mail-order prescription drug programs to save money on prescription medications.

Review medical bills and insurance statements carefully to ensure accuracy and identify any errors or discrepancies.

Negotiate with healthcare providers or insurance companies to reduce costs when possible.

Explore cost-saving strategies, such as healthcare discount programs, flexible spending accounts (FSAs), and health savings accounts (HSAs), to help offset out-of-pocket expenses and lower overall healthcare costs.

By estimating healthcare needs, understanding Medicare coverage, exploring supplemental coverage options, and managing healthcare costs effectively, you can plan and budget for healthcare expenses in your final third of life with confidence and peace of mind. Taking proactive steps to protect your health and financial well-being can help ensure a comfortable and secure retirement.

Reflection and Review

1. What are the different parts of Medicare, and what do they cover?

Medicare has four parts: Part A (hospital insurance), Part B (medical insurance), Part C (Medicare Advantage), and Part D (prescription drug coverage).

2. How can you maximize/optimize your Social Security benefits?

Strategies include delaying benefits, coordinating benefits with a spouse, and understanding the impact of working in retirement as well as seeking advice from a Registered Social Security Analyst.

3. What are some common misconceptions about Medicare, and how can you avoid them?

Misconceptions include assuming Medicare covers all healthcare costs and that you're automatically enrolled at age 65. Education and research can help clarify these misunderstandings.

4. What is the difference between Medicare Advantage and Original Medicare?

Medicare Advantage plans are offered by private insurance companies and provide coverage beyond what Original Medicare offers, often including prescription drug coverage and additional benefits.

5. How can you plan for out-of-pocket healthcare expenses in retirement?

Planning involves estimating healthcare costs, exploring supplemental coverage options, and considering long-term care insurance.

Reflection

Take a moment to reflect on the insights and lessons you've gained from this section.

Consider how you can apply this knowledge to your own life and plans for the future.

Use this space to jot down your thoughts, ideas, and action steps as you continue on your journey towards a fulfilling retirement.

Moving on...

Having gained clarity on navigating the complexities of Social Security benefits and healthcare coverage through Medicare, we now turn our attention to another pivotal aspect of retirement planning: the transition to a new living space.

As we've explored in the previous sections, understanding your entitlements and options for healthcare coverage in retirement is essential for ensuring financial security and peace of mind. However, the decision to downsize or relocate to a new home presents additional considerations and opportunities for optimizing your retirement lifestyle.

In the following section, we dive into the practicalities of real estate downsizing and relocation, offering insights, strategies, and practical advice to help you make informed decisions about your living arrangements in retirement.

From rightsizing your living space to tips for a smooth relocation and making your new home your haven, this section provides invaluable guidance for navigating the transition to a new chapter of life with confidence and ease.

So let us embark on this journey together, armed with the knowledge and resources to navigate the complexities of real estate downsizing and relocation with clarity, purpose, and excitement.

By embracing change and embracing the opportunities it brings, you can create a living environment that supports your evolving needs and enriches your retirement experience for years to come.

"Home is a place you grow up wanting to leave and grow old wanting to get back to."

- John Ed Pearce

Section IV: Real Estate Downsizing & Relocation

This section addresses the practical aspects of real estate downsizing and relocation, offering guidance on rightsizing your living space, planning a smooth relocation, and making your new home a haven in "Your Final Third", emphasizing the importance of thoughtful planning and decision-making in retirement.

Rightsizing Your Living Space

As you enter "Your Final Third", downsizing your living space can offer numerous benefits, including reduced maintenance, lower expenses, and greater flexibility.

In this sub-section, we'll explore the concept of "rightsizing" and provide guidance on evaluating your current housing needs and finding a home that better suits your lifestyle and budget.

Whether you're looking to move to a smaller house, condo, or senior living community, we'll discuss strategies for decluttering, organizing, and transitioning to a more manageable living situation.

"Rightsizing" is the process of evaluating your current housing situation and making adjustments to find a home that better suits your lifestyle, needs, and budget as you enter "Your Final Third".

Here's further explanation and guidance on rightsizing, including evaluating your housing needs, finding a more suitable home, and strategies for decluttering, organizing, and transitioning to a more manageable living situation:

1. Evaluate Your Current Housing Needs

Assess your current living situation, including the size, layout, and features of your home, as well as any challenges or limitations you may encounter.

Consider factors such as accessibility, maintenance requirements, proximity to amenities and healthcare services, and overall comfort and convenience.

Reflect on your future lifestyle preferences and anticipated changes in health, mobility, and social activities as you age.

2. Find a Home That "Better Suits" Your Lifestyle and Budget

 Research different housing options that align with your needs and preferences, such as downsizing to a smaller home, moving to a retirement community or senior living facility, or exploring age-friendly housing options.

Consider factors such as location, amenities, affordability, and proximity to family and support networks when evaluating potential housing options.

Work with a real estate agent or senior relocation specialist who understands your needs and can help you find a home that meets your criteria and fits within your budget.

Feel free to reach out to *Senior Solutions Today* for assistance and/or guidance, www.seniorsolutionstoday.com

Buy for Less

Buying a home is the single biggest financial decision you will make in your life. You need a top local agent who knows that market and can help you quickly identify top candidates.

When you find the perfect home, you need an experienced professional with strong negotiation skills who can help you write a winning offer at the lowest price possible.

Sell For More

With rapidly changing home values, increased regulations, and numerous marketing options, you need an experienced professional who understands your market, knows how to bring the best out of your property, and is willing to do what it takes to sell your home for the highest price possible.

As a Relocation Specialist, I belong to a nationwide network of 90,000 top-rated agents serving every zip code in all 50 states.

Instead of helping you buy or sell a home personally, I help match my clients with up to 3 great agents who specialize in your market.

The best part? This is a 100% FREE service, so there is no cost, pressure or obligation! With my experience and connections, I can quickly help you find the perfect agent better than what most people are able to do on their own.

3. Declutter, Organize, and Transition Effectively

Start by decluttering your current home and sorting through belongings to determine what to keep, donate, sell, or discard.

Focus on decluttering one area at a time, such as closets, cabinets, or rooms, and enlist help from family members or professional organizers if needed.

Prioritize items that are essential or hold sentimental value and consider downsizing possessions to fit into your new living space.

Develop a plan for organizing and packing belongings, labeling boxes, and coordinating logistics for moving to your new home.

Take the opportunity to streamline your possessions and create a more simplified and organized living environment that enhances your quality of life and reduces stress.

4. Adjust and Adapt to Your New Living Situation

Give yourself time to adjust to your new home and neighborhood and be patient with the transition process.

Explore opportunities to get involved in social activities, clubs, or community events in your new area to meet neighbors and build connections.

Seek support from family, friends, or local resources to help with the transition and address any challenges or concerns that arise.

Stay flexible and open-minded as you settle into your new living situation and be willing to make adjustments as needed to ensure your comfort and satisfaction.

In conclusion, rightsizing involves evaluating your current housing needs, finding a home that better suits your lifestyle and budget, and transitioning effectively to a more manageable living situation as you enter your final third of life.

By decluttering, organizing, and adapting to your new home, you can create a living environment that enhances your quality of life and supports your overall well-being in retirement.

Tips for Smooth Relocation

Moving can be a daunting task at any age, but proper planning can help ensure a smooth transition to your new home.

In this sub-section, we'll provide practical tips and advice for planning and executing a successful relocation in "Your Final Third".

Whether you're moving across town or across the country, we'll help you navigate the logistics and settle into your new home with ease.

Planning and executing a successful relocation in your final third of life requires careful preparation, organization, and attention to detail.

Here are practical tips and advice for a smooth transition, from hiring professional movers to creating a timeline and checklist, minimizing stress, maximizing efficiency, and settling into your new home with ease:

1. Hiring Professional Movers...No DIY Please!

Let's face it, "Do It Yourself" was once an option. In those days we had better bodies, no money and friends we could bribe with a beverage.

But those days are in the past, and we have accumulated way too much "stuff" to fit into that little trailer we used to rent. So let's splurge a little, go "professional", and keep our medical "co-pays" in our pocket.

Research and interview multiple moving companies to compare services, rates, and customer reviews.

Choose a reputable moving company with experience in senior relocation and a track record of reliable service.

Request a detailed estimate in writing and inquire about insurance coverage, packing materials, and any additional services offered.

2. Creating a Timeline and Checklist

Start planning your move well in advance to allow ample time for preparations and arrangements.

Create a moving timeline and checklist to outline tasks and deadlines leading up to your moving day.

Break down tasks into manageable steps, such as decluttering, packing, arranging for utilities and mail forwarding, and scheduling moving services.

3. Minimizing Stress and Maximizing Efficiency

Declutter and downsize belongings before packing to reduce the volume of items to be moved and simplify the moving process.

Pack systematically, room by room, and label boxes clearly to facilitate unpacking and organization at your new home.

Create an essentials box with important documents, medications, toiletries, and other items you'll need immediately upon arrival at your new home.

Communicate with your moving company and coordinate logistics, such as parking arrangements, elevator access, and any special requirements or instructions for moving day.

4. Navigating the Logistics

Arrange for utilities to be disconnected at your current home and connected at your new home on moving day to ensure a seamless transition.

Notify relevant parties of your change of address, including utility providers, financial institutions, healthcare providers, and government agencies.

Forward your mail to your new address through the USPS and update your contact information with subscriptions, memberships, and other services.

5. Settling into Your New Home with Ease

Unpack and organize essentials first, focusing on setting up key areas such as the bedroom, kitchen, and bathroom.

Take time to explore your new neighborhood and familiarize yourself with local amenities, services, and points of interest.

Meet your neighbors and introduce yourself to build connections and establish a sense of community.

Take breaks as needed and prioritize self-care throughout the moving process to reduce stress and maintain your well-being.

By following these practical tips and advice, you can plan and execute a successful relocation in "Your Final Third", minimizing stress, maximizing efficiency, and settling into your new home with ease.

With careful preparation and organization, you can make the transition to your new living situation a positive and rewarding experience.

Making Your New Home Your Haven

Your new home is more than just a place to live; it's a sanctuary where you can thrive in "Your Final Third".

In this sub-section, we'll explore ways to personalize and optimize your living space to enhance comfort, convenience, and enjoyment.

From interior design tips to home safety and accessibility modifications, we'll discuss strategies for making your new home a haven that reflects your unique needs and preferences.

Whether you're downsizing to a smaller space or transitioning to a retirement community, we'll help you create a living environment that supports your well-being and enriches your retirement years.

Personalizing and optimizing your living space in "Your Final Third" is essential for creating a home that enhances comfort, convenience, and enjoyment while supporting your well-being and enriching your retirement years.

Here are ways to personalize and optimize your living space, from interior design tips to home safety and accessibility modifications:

1. Interior Design Tips

Choose furniture and decor that prioritizes comfort, functionality, and ease of use, such as ergonomic seating, adjustable lighting, and storage solutions.

Incorporate elements that reflect your personal style, interests, and memories, such as family photos, artwork, and souvenirs from travels.

Use color and texture to create a warm and inviting atmosphere, incorporating calming hues and soft fabrics to promote relaxation and tranquility.

Optimize natural light and ventilation to brighten your living space and improve indoor air quality, using curtains or blinds for privacy and temperature control.

2. Home Safety and Accessibility Modifications

Conduct a home safety assessment to identify potential hazards and areas for improvement, such as uneven flooring, inadequate lighting, and tripping hazards.

Install grab bars, handrails, and nonslip surfaces in bathrooms and other high-risk areas to prevent falls and enhance accessibility.

Consider installing smart home technology, such as motion-sensor lighting, remote-controlled thermostats, and home security systems, for added safety and convenience.

Make adjustments to accommodate changing mobility and physical needs, such as widening doorways, lowering countertops, and installing stairlifts or ramps as needed.

3. Creating a Haven That Reflects Your Unique Needs and Preferences

Designate specific areas of your home for relaxation, hobbies, and socializing, incorporating comfortable seating, task lighting, and storage solutions tailored to your activities and interests.

Personalize your living space with meaningful items and mementos that bring you joy and evoke positive memories, such as family heirlooms, favorite books, and cherished keepsakes.

Create a sensory-rich environment with plants, aromatherapy, and soothing sounds to promote relaxation and reduce stress.

Embrace technology and innovation to enhance your daily life, incorporating smart home devices, assistive technology, and entertainment systems that cater to your needs and preferences.

4. Creating a Living Environment That Supports Your Well-being

Prioritize comfort and functionality in your living space, ensuring that furniture, fixtures, and layout promote ease of movement and accessibility.

Foster a sense of connection and community by hosting gatherings, events, or activities that bring family, friends, and neighbors together.

Cultivate a healthy lifestyle by incorporating wellness practices into your daily routine, such as exercise, meditation, and nutritious eating habits.

Maintain a clean, clutter-free environment to promote mental clarity, reduce stress, and enhance overall well-being.

By personalizing and optimizing your living space to reflect your unique needs and preferences, you can create a haven that supports your well-being and enriches your retirement years.

With thoughtful design, safety modifications, and a focus on comfort and functionality, you can enjoy a fulfilling and rewarding living environment that enhances your quality of life and brings you joy and satisfaction in your later years.

Reflection and Review

1. What are some reasons for downsizing or relocating in retirement?

Reasons include reducing expenses, simplifying lifestyle, moving closer to family, or downsizing to a more manageable home.

2. What are some tips for preparing for a smooth relocation?

Tips include decluttering and organizing belongings, researching new neighborhoods, hiring professional movers, and creating a moving timeline.

3. How can you make your new home feel like a haven in retirement?

Suggestions include personalizing your space, creating a comfortable and functional layout, and incorporating elements that promote relaxation and well-being.

4. What are the financial considerations when downsizing or relocating in retirement?

Considerations include selling your current home, budgeting for moving expenses, and evaluating the cost of living in your new location.

5. How can you navigate the emotional aspects of downsizing or relocating?

Strategies include acknowledging and managing emotions, focusing on the positive aspects of the move, and staying connected with loved ones throughout the process.

Reflection

Take a moment to reflect on the insights and lessons you've gained from this section.

Consider how you can apply this knowledge to your own life and plans for the future.

Use this space to jot down your thoughts, ideas, and action steps as you continue on your journey towards a fulfilling retirement.

Moving on...

As we've explored the practicalities of rightsizing your living space and making a smooth transition to a new home, we now turn our attention to another critical aspect of retirement planning: safeguarding your assets and ensuring your legacy through comprehensive estate planning.

While the decision to downsize or relocate may involve logistical considerations and lifestyle adjustments, it also presents an opportune moment to revisit your legal documents and estate plans to ensure they reflect your current wishes and circumstances.

From wills and trusts to powers of attorney and advance directives, these legal instruments play a crucial role in protecting your interests and preserving your legacy for future generations.

In the following section, we delve into the intricacies of estate planning, offering insights, strategies, and practical advice to help you navigate the complexities of legal documentation and ensure your affairs are in order.

Whether you're updating existing documents or creating new ones, this section provides invaluable guidance for safeguarding your assets, minimizing taxes, and establishing a framework for the orderly distribution of your estate.

So let us embark on this next phase of our journey together, armed with the knowledge and resources to navigate the legal intricacies of estate planning with clarity, confidence, and peace of mind.

By taking proactive steps to protect your legacy and provide for your loved ones, you can leave a lasting impact that extends far beyond your lifetime.

"The legacy we leave is not just in our possessions, but in the quality of our lives."

- Billy Graham

Section V: Legal Documents & Estate Planning

This section addresses the importance of legal documents and estate planning in ensuring your wishes are carried out and your legacy is preserved in Your Final Third, emphasizing the importance of comprehensive planning for retirement and beyond.

Importance of Wills and Trusts

Wills and trusts are fundamental components of estate planning, providing a roadmap for how your assets will be distributed upon your passing.

In this sub-section, we'll explore the importance of having a will and/or trust in place and discuss the differences between the two.

We'll cover essential elements to include in your will or trust, such as naming beneficiaries, appointing guardians for minor children, and specifying funeral arrangements.

We'll also discuss the role of a personal representative or trustee and provide guidance on updating your estate plan as circumstances change.

Having a will and/or trust in place is essential for ensuring that your wishes are carried out and your assets are distributed according to your preferences after your passing.

Here's an exploration of the importance of wills and trusts, along with guidance on essential elements to include and updating your estate plan:

1. Importance of Wills and Trusts

Wills and Trusts are legal documents that allow you to specify how you want your assets to be distributed upon your death.

A Will provides instructions for the distribution of your assets and the appointment of guardians for minor children, while a Trust allows you to transfer assets to beneficiaries and manage them according to specific terms and conditions.

Having a Will and/or Trust in place ensures that your wishes are legally documented and can help prevent disputes among family members and beneficiaries.

2. Differences Between Wills and Trusts

A Will takes effect upon your death and is subject to probate, the legal process of administering your estate and distributing assets according to your will.

A Trust, on the other hand, is created during your lifetime and can be used to hold and manage assets for the benefit of beneficiaries.

Trust assets are typically not subject to probate, which can help streamline the estate administration process and maintain privacy.

3. Essential Elements to Include in Your Will or Trust

Naming Beneficiaries:

Specify who will inherit your assets, including family members, friends, charities, or other beneficiaries.

Appointing Guardians for Minor Children:

Designate individuals or couples to care for your minor children in the event of your death or incapacity.

Specifying Funeral Arrangements:

Outline your preferences for funeral or memorial services, burial or cremation, and any other final arrangements.

Appointing a Personal Representative or Trustee:

Choose someone you trust to administer your estate or trust and carry out your wishes according to the terms of your will or trust document.

4. Guidance on Updating Your Estate Plan

Review your estate plan periodically to ensure that it reflects your current wishes, circumstances, and preferences.

Update your will or trust as needed to accommodate major life events, such as marriage, divorce, birth or adoption of children, or significant changes in assets or financial situation.

Consider consulting with an estate planning attorney or financial advisor to review your estate plan and make updates or revisions as necessary to ensure that it remains valid and effective.

In conclusion, having a will and/or trust in place is essential for ensuring that your wishes are carried out and your assets are distributed according to your preferences after your passing.

By including essential elements in your will or trust, such as naming beneficiaries, appointing guardians for minor children, and specifying funeral arrangements, you can create a comprehensive estate plan that provides clarity and peace of mind for you and your loved ones.

Regularly updating your estate plan as circumstances change ensures that it remains current and reflects your current wishes and circumstances.

Powers of Attorney: Planning for Incapacity

Planning for incapacity is a critical aspect of estate planning, ensuring that your financial and healthcare decisions are managed according to your wishes if you become unable to make them yourself.

In this sub-section, we'll discuss the importance of powers of attorney and advance directives and explain how they work to appoint trusted individuals to act on your behalf in the event of incapacity.

We'll explore the different types of Powers of Attorney, including Financial Power of Attorney and Healthcare Power of Attorney, and provide guidance on choosing the right agents to represent your interests.

Powers of Attorney and Advance Directives are essential legal documents that allow you to appoint trusted individuals to act on your behalf in the event of incapacity.

Here's a further discussion of their importance, how they work, the different types available, and guidance on choosing the right agents to represent your interests:

1. Importance of Powers of Attorney and Advance Directives

Powers of Attorney and Advance Directives empower you to designate trusted individuals to make financial and healthcare decisions on your behalf if you become incapacitated and are unable to make decisions for yourself.

Without these documents in place, decisions about your medical care and financial affairs may be made by others without your input, potentially leading to disputes or uncertainty about your wishes.

2. How They Work

A Power of Attorney is a legal document that grants authority to another person (known as an Agent or Attorney-in-Fact) to act on your behalf in financial or legal matters.

An Advance Directive is a legal document that outlines your preferences for medical treatment and appoints a Healthcare Agent to make healthcare decisions for you if you are unable to do so.

Powers of Attorney and Advance Directives only take effect if you become incapacitated and are unable to make decisions for yourself.

They remain in effect until revoked or until your death.

3. Different Types of Powers of Attorney

Financial Power of Attorney:

This document authorizes your chosen agent to manage your financial affairs, including paying bills, managing investments, and making legal decisions on your behalf.

Healthcare Power of Attorney:

This document appoints a trusted individual to make healthcare decisions for you if you are unable to do so, including choices about medical treatments, surgeries, and end-of-life care.

4. Guidance on Choosing the Right Agents

Select agents who are trustworthy, reliable, and capable of acting in your best interests, even under challenging circumstances.

Consider individuals who understand your values, preferences, and healthcare wishes and who are willing to advocate for your needs and wishes.

Discuss your wishes and expectations with your chosen agents beforehand to ensure they understand your preferences and are prepared to fulfill their responsibilities if called upon.

Choose alternate agents or successors in case your primary agents are unable or unwilling to act when needed.

In conclusion, powers of attorney and advance directives are essential legal documents that allow you to appoint trusted individuals to act on your behalf in the event of incapacity.

By creating these documents and selecting the right agents to represent your interests, you can ensure that your wishes are respected, and your affairs are managed according to your preferences, even if you are unable to make decisions for yourself.

It's important to discuss your wishes with your chosen agents and periodically review and update these documents as needed to reflect any changes in your circumstances or preferences.

Ensuring Your Legacy

Your legacy is more than just the assets you leave behind; it's the impact you've made on the world and the memories you've created with loved ones.

In this sub-section, we'll explore ways to ensure your legacy lives on in a meaningful and lasting way.

From documenting your life story to preserving family traditions and values, we'll discuss strategies for passing down your legacy to future generations.

We'll also address the importance of communicating your wishes to your loved ones and involving them in the estate planning process to minimize conflicts and ensure your legacy is honored according to your wishes.

Ensuring your legacy lives on in a meaningful and lasting way involves more than just passing down material possessions; it's about preserving your life story, values, and traditions for future generations.

Here are ways to accomplish this, along with strategies for passing down your legacy and the importance of involving your loved ones in the estate planning process:

1. Documenting Your Life Story

Write a memoir or autobiography to document your life experiences, memories, and lessons learned.

Record oral histories or interviews with family members to capture their stories and perspectives.

Create a family history or genealogy to trace your ancestry and preserve your family's heritage.

2. Preserving Family Traditions and Values

Identify and document important family traditions, rituals, and values that are meaningful to you and your loved ones.

Share stories and anecdotes about family traditions and the significance behind them.

Create opportunities for family members to participate in and contribute to family traditions, fostering a sense of connection and continuity across generations.

3. Passing Down Your Legacy

Identify meaningful heirlooms, keepsakes, and mementos to pass down to future generations, along with stories and memories associated with each item.

Establish a family legacy project or foundation to support causes or organizations that are important to you and reflect your values.

Consider creating a digital legacy, such as a website or online memorial, to share photos, videos, and stories with family members and future generations.

4. Communicating Your Wishes to Loved Ones

Have open and honest conversations with your loved ones about your values, wishes, and expectations for the future.

Discuss your estate planning documents, including your will, trust, powers of attorney, and advance directives, with family members to ensure they understand your wishes and their roles in carrying them out.

Encourage family members to ask questions and share their perspectives, fostering transparency and understanding among all parties involved.

5. Involving Loved Ones in the Estate Planning Process

Involve your loved ones in the estate planning process by soliciting their input and feedback on important decisions, such as the distribution of assets, guardianship arrangements, and charitable giving.

Consider appointing family members as executors, trustees, or agents under your powers of attorney, if appropriate, and discuss their roles and responsibilities in advance.

Address any potential conflicts or concerns proactively by discussing them openly and seeking mutually agreeable solutions.

By documenting your life story, preserving family traditions and values, passing down your legacy, communicating your wishes to your loved ones, and involving them in the estate planning process, you can ensure that your legacy lives on in a meaningful and lasting way.

By doing so, you can leave behind a legacy that not only honors your memory but also enriches the lives of future generations.

Reflection and Review

1. Why is it important to have a will or trust in place?

Wills and trusts help ensure your assets are distributed according to your wishes, minimize estate taxes, and provide for minor children or dependents.

2. What are the differences between a power of attorney and an advance directive?

A power of attorney authorizes someone to make financial or legal decisions on your behalf, while an advance directive outlines your preferences for medical treatment in the event you are unable to communicate.

3. How can you ensure your legacy is preserved for future generations?

Suggestions include documenting your life story, preserving family traditions and heirlooms, and communicating your values and wishes to loved ones.

4. What are the potential consequences of not having an estate plan in place?

Consequences may include your assets being distributed according to state law, potential disputes among family members, and increased taxes or probate costs.

5. How often should you review and update your estate plan?

It's recommended to review your estate plan regularly, especially after major life events such as marriage, divorce, or other major life events that warrant a review and potential update of your estate plan, such as:

Birth or adoption of a child or grandchild

Death of a spouse or beneficiary

Significant changes in financial status, such as inheritance or windfall

Relocation to another state or country with different legal requirements

Changes in tax laws or regulations affecting estate planning

Changes in health status or long-term care needs

Starting or selling a business

Changes in personal or charitable goals and preferences

Reflection

Take a moment to reflect on the insights and lessons you've gained from this section.

Consider how you can apply this knowledge to your own life and plans for the future.

Use this space to jot down your thoughts, ideas, and action steps as you continue on your journey towards a fulfilling retirement.

Moving on...

With our legal affairs in order and our legacy secured, we now turn our attention to another vital aspect of retirement living fostering meaningful connections and building a vibrant community around us.

While estate planning may focus on the practicalities of asset protection and inheritance, the true richness of retirement lies in the relationships we cultivate and the communities we nurture.

As we embark on this next phase of our journey, let us recognize the profound impact that social connections and community engagement have on our overall well-being and quality of life.

In the following section, we dive into the importance of embracing community and fostering social connections in retirement, offering insights, strategies, and practical advice to help you build and maintain meaningful relationships.

From joining clubs and organizations to volunteering and giving back to your community, this section explores the myriad ways you can connect with others and make a positive impact in the world around you.

So let us embark on this journey together, armed with the knowledge and inspiration to cultivate a rich and fulfilling social life in retirement.

By reaching out, getting involved, and building bridges with others, you can create a supportive network of friends and allies who enrich your life and accompany you on this exciting adventure of retirement living.

As we nurture these connections, it's important to remember that retirement is a time of renewal—a chance to rediscover who we are and what truly matters. Social engagement helps us stay grounded and feel relevant, combating the feelings of isolation that can sometimes accompany this stage of life. It's not just about surrounding ourselves with others but finding those connections that inspire us, challenge us to grow, and fill our days with laughter, empathy, and shared experiences. Friendships and community bonds act as anchors, providing stability and encouragement as we navigate the evolving landscape of our later years.

The beauty of this phase is that it offers the flexibility to curate your social life in ways that work best for you. Whether you're an introvert or extrovert, whether you prefer intimate gatherings or larger social events, retirement presents the perfect opportunity to shape your days around the types of interactions that fulfill you. This might mean deepening existing relationships with family and old friends, or it could mean stepping outside your comfort zone to meet new people who share your interests and values. The key is to remain open to new experiences and embrace the unexpected connections that can lead to lifelong friendships.

Ultimately, building a community in retirement goes beyond the simple joy of companionship—it strengthens your emotional resilience, boosts your mental and physical health, and adds layers of richness to your life. The shared experiences, the mutual support, and the sense of belonging that comes from these relationships all contribute to a vibrant, purposeful retirement. By actively cultivating these connections, you create a dynamic environment where you not only thrive but also help others flourish, leaving behind a legacy of kindness, engagement, and meaningful impact on the lives of those you've touched.

"We don't stop playing because we grow old; we grow old because we stop playing."

- George Bernard Shaw

Section VI: Embracing Community & Social Connections

This section emphasizes the importance of community and social connections in enhancing quality of life and overall well-being in the final third of life emphasizing the importance of holistic well-being in retirement.

Building and Maintaining Social Networks

Social connections play a crucial role in maintaining health, happiness, and overall well-being, especially as you enter "Your Final Third".

In this sub-section, we'll discuss the importance of building and maintaining social networks and provide practical tips for staying connected with friends, family, and community.

From joining clubs and organizations to participating in social events and activities, we'll explore strategies for fostering meaningful relationships and combating social isolation.

We'll also discuss the benefits of technology and social media for staying connected, particularly for seniors who may face physical limitations or mobility challenges.

Building and maintaining social networks is crucial for overall well-being, particularly in later life when social connections can provide support, companionship, and a sense of belonging.

Here's an expansion on the importance of social networks and practical tips for staying connected with friends, family, and community:

1. Joining Clubs and Organizations

Participate in local clubs, organizations, or hobby groups that align with your interests and passions.

Join community centers, senior centers, or religious institutions that offer social activities, classes, and events for older adults.

Explore online communities and forums related to your hobbies, interests, or life experiences to connect with like-minded individuals.

2. Participating in Social Events and Activities

Attend social gatherings, community events, and cultural activities in your area to meet new people and expand your social circle.

Host gatherings or dinner parties at your home to bring friends and family together for shared experiences and meaningful conversations.

Volunteer for local charities or organizations that allow you to give back to your community while connecting with others who share your values and interests.

3. Fostering Meaningful Relationships

Prioritize quality over quantity when it comes to social connections, focusing on nurturing relationships that bring joy, support, and fulfillment into your life.

Make an effort to stay in touch with friends and family regularly, whether through phone calls, video chats, or in-person visits.

Listen actively, show empathy, and express appreciation for the people in your life, fostering deeper connections and mutual understanding.

4. Combating Social Isolation

Be proactive about reaching out to others and initiating social interactions, especially if you're feeling lonely or isolated.

Seek out support groups or counseling services if you're struggling with feelings of loneliness or depression, and don't hesitate to ask for help when needed.

Stay engaged in meaningful activities and hobbies that bring you joy and fulfillment, even if you're unable to participate in social events as frequently as you'd like.

5. The Benefits of Technology and Social Media

Embrace technology and social media as tools for staying connected with friends and family, particularly if you're facing physical limitations or mobility challenges.

Use video calling platforms, messaging apps, and social networking sites to communicate with loved ones, share updates, and participate in virtual social gatherings.

Explore online learning platforms, virtual events, and digital communities that allow you to connect with others and pursue your interests from the comfort of your own home.

By building and maintaining social networks, participating in social events and activities, fostering meaningful relationships, and leveraging technology and social media, you can combat social isolation and stay connected with others, enhancing your overall well-being and quality of life in later life.

Cultivating strong social connections can provide support, companionship, and a sense of purpose, enriching your retirement years and promoting a fulfilling life.

Volunteering and Giving Back

Volunteering and giving back to your community can bring a sense of purpose, fulfillment, and connection in "Your Final Third".

In this sub-section, we'll explore the benefits of volunteering and provide guidance on finding opportunities that align with your interests, skills, and schedule.

Whether you're mentoring youth, serving meals at a soup kitchen, or participating in environmental conservation efforts, we'll discuss the many ways you can make a positive impact and leave a lasting legacy through volunteer work.

We'll also address the physical and mental health benefits of altruism and the importance of finding a balance between giving and self-care.

Volunteering offers a multitude of benefits,

both for the individuals being served and for the volunteers themselves.

Here's an expansion on the benefits of volunteering, guidance on finding opportunities, and the importance of balancing altruism with self-care:

1. Benefits of Volunteering

A Sense of Purpose

Volunteering provides a sense of purpose and fulfillment by contributing to causes and communities that are meaningful to you.

Social Connection

Volunteering allows you to connect with like-minded individuals and build meaningful relationships with people who share your values and interests.

Skill Development

Volunteering offers opportunities to develop new skills, gain valuable experience, and expand your knowledge in various areas.

Physical and Mental Health

Volunteering has been linked to improved physical health, reduced stress levels, and increased happiness and life satisfaction.

Community Impact

Volunteering enables you to make a positive impact on your community and contribute to positive social change.

2. Finding Opportunities That Align with Your Interests and Skills

Assess Your Interests

Consider your passions, hobbies, and areas of expertise when exploring volunteer opportunities.

Research Organizations

Research local nonprofits, charities, and community organizations that align with your interests and values.

Reach Out!

Contact organizations directly to inquire about volunteer opportunities and express your interest in getting involved.

Consider Your Schedule

Look for volunteer opportunities that fit your schedule and availability, whether it's a one-time event, a recurring commitment, or a flexible arrangement.

3. Ways to Make a Positive Impact Through Volunteer Work

Mentoring Youth

Volunteer as a mentor or tutor for young people, offering guidance, support, and encouragement to help them reach their full potential.

Serving Meals

Volunteer at a soup kitchen, food pantry, or homeless shelter to provide meals and assistance to individuals and families in need.

Environmental Conservation

Get involved in environmental conservation efforts by volunteering for clean-up events, tree planting projects, or wildlife habitat restoration initiatives.

4. Physical and Mental Health Benefits of Altruism

Reduced Stress

Volunteering can help reduce stress levels and promote relaxation by providing a sense of purpose and fulfillment.

Increased Happiness

Giving back to others through volunteering has been shown to increase happiness and life satisfaction.

Improved Physical Health

Volunteering has been associated with improved physical health outcomes, including lower blood pressure, reduced risk of chronic diseases, and increased longevity.

Enhanced Social Connection

Volunteering fosters social connections and a sense of belonging, which are important factors for overall well-being and mental health.

5. Finding Balance Between Giving and Self-Care

Set Boundaries

Establish boundaries and prioritize self-care to prevent burnout and maintain balance in your life.

Listen to Your Needs

Pay attention to your physical and emotional well-being, and don't hesitate to take breaks or step back from volunteering if needed.

Practice Self-Compassion

Be kind to yourself and recognize that it's okay to prioritize your own needs and well-being while still giving back to others.

Find Joy in Giving

Focus on the joy and fulfillment that volunteering brings, and remember that by taking care of yourself, you're better able to make a positive impact on others.

By finding volunteer opportunities that align with your interests, skills, and schedule, you can make a positive impact on your community while experiencing the physical and mental health benefits of altruism.

Just remember to prioritize self-care and find balance between giving to others and taking care of yourself, ensuring that your volunteer work remains sustainable and fulfilling in the long term.

Finding Meaningful Connections

Meaningful connections enrich our lives and provide a sense of belonging and support, particularly as we age.

In this sub-section, we'll explore strategies for finding and nurturing meaningful connections in "Your Final Third".

From deepening relationships with existing friends and family members to forging new connections through shared interests and experiences, we'll discuss practical tips for building authentic and fulfilling relationships.

We'll also address the importance of communication, empathy, and active listening in fostering meaningful connections and strengthening social bonds.

By prioritizing relationships and investing in meaningful connections, you can cultivate a support network that enhances your well-being and enriches your retirement years.

In your final third of life, nurturing meaningful connections is essential for overall well-being and fulfillment.

Here's an expansion on strategies for finding and nurturing meaningful connections, practical tips for building authentic relationships, and the importance of communication, empathy, and active listening:

1. Deepening Relationships with Existing Friends and Family

Make time for regular contact with friends and family members, whether through phone calls, video chats, or in-person visits.

Share meaningful experiences and memories with loved ones, such as attending events together, taking trips, or engaging in shared hobbies and interests.

Express appreciation and gratitude for the important people in your life, letting them know how much they mean to you.

2. Forging New Connections Through Shared Interests and Experiences

Pursue activities and hobbies that interest you and offer opportunities for social interaction, such as joining clubs, classes, or community groups.

Attend social events, gatherings, and networking opportunities in your area to meet new people and expand your social circle.

Volunteer for causes or organizations that align with your interests and values, connecting with like-minded individuals who share your passions.

3. Practical Tips for Building Authentic Relationships

Be yourself and be genuine in your interactions with others, allowing your true personality and values to shine through.

Show interest in others by asking questions, listening attentively, and showing empathy and understanding.

Share your own thoughts, feelings, and experiences openly and honestly, fostering trust and mutual respect in your relationships.

Be reliable and dependable in your interactions with others, following through on commitments and offering support when needed.

4. Importance of Communication, Empathy, and Active Listening

Practice effective communication skills, including clear expression of thoughts and feelings, active listening, and empathy for others' perspectives.

Be present and engaged in conversations, giving your full attention to the person you're speaking with and demonstrating genuine interest in what they have to say.

Show empathy and compassion for others by acknowledging their feelings, validating their experiences, and offering support and encouragement.

Practice active listening by focusing on the speaker's words, asking clarifying questions, and summarizing their points to ensure understanding.

By finding and nurturing meaningful connections in your final third of life, you can enrich your relationships, enhance your sense of belonging, and experience greater joy and fulfillment in your daily life.

Whether deepening existing relationships with friends and family members or forging new connections through shared interests and experiences, prioritizing communication, empathy, and active listening can help strengthen social bonds and foster authentic and fulfilling relationships that contribute to your overall well-being and happiness.

Reflection and Review

1. Why is social connection important for overall well-being in retirement?

Social connection promotes mental and emotional health, reduces feelings of loneliness and isolation, and provides a sense of belonging and purpose.

2. What are some strategies for building and maintaining social networks in retirement?

Strategies include joining clubs or groups based on shared interests, participating in community events or activities, volunteering, and staying in touch with friends and family.

3. How can technology and social media help seniors stay connected with others?

Technology and social media platforms can facilitate communication, allow seniors to connect with distant loved ones, and provide access to online communities and support groups.

4. What are the benefits of intergenerational connections in retirement?

Intergenerational connections provide opportunities for learning, mentorship, and mutual support, as well as fostering a sense of continuity and passing on wisdom and traditions to future generations.

5. How can retirees combat social isolation and loneliness?

Retirees can combat social isolation and loneliness by actively seeking out social opportunities, reaching out to others, participating in group activities, and staying engaged in their communities.

Reflection

Take a moment to reflect on the insights and lessons you've gained from this section.

Consider how you can apply this knowledge to your own life and plans for the future.

Use this space to jot down your thoughts, ideas, and action steps as you continue on your journey towards a fulfilling retirement.

Moving on...

As we've explored the profound impact of community and social connections on our retirement journey, we now arrive at the culmination of our exploration: the invitation to embrace the fullness of life and live our best lives in the final third.

Through the sections preceding this conclusion, we've delved into the practicalities of retirement planning, from financial preparedness and healthcare considerations to legal documentation and estate planning.

We've also celebrated the importance of personal growth, physical well-being, and social engagement in creating a fulfilling retirement experience.

Now, as we stand at the threshold of this new section, let us pause to reflect on the journey thus far and the opportunities that lie ahead.

Retirement is not merely a destination but a dynamic process of self-discovery, growth, and exploration. It is a chance to reinvent ourselves, pursue our passions, and make a meaningful impact in the world around us.

In the pages that follow, we offer a heartfelt invitation to embrace the possibilities of "Your Final Third" with open arms and an adventurous spirit.

By harnessing the lessons learned, the connections made, and the dreams yet to be realized, we can chart a course toward a future filled with purpose, vitality, and joy.

So let us step boldly into this next phase of our journey, empowered by the knowledge that we hold the keys to our own happiness and fulfillment.

By living authentically, connecting deeply, and embracing the richness of each moment, we can truly savor the gift of life and experience the fullness of our potential in the "Final Third".

*"It's not the years in your life that count.
It's the life in your years."*

- Abraham Lincoln

Conclusion: Living Your **<u>Best Life</u>** in the Final Third

As you reach the conclusion of this guide, you've embarked on a journey of exploration, preparation, and empowerment for "Your Final Third" of life.

You've gained insights into various aspects of aging, from personal development and financial planning to healthcare and social connections.

Now, it's time to reflect on the key takeaways and commit to living your best life in the years ahead.

Throughout this book, you've learned the importance of embracing the opportunities and challenges that come with aging, reframing your mindset to view "Your Final Third" as a time of growth and fulfillment.

You've discovered practical strategies for staying physically and mentally active, managing your finances, navigating healthcare decisions, and fostering meaningful connections with others.

You've also gained valuable knowledge about legal documents and estate planning, ensuring your wishes are carried out and your legacy is preserved.

As you move forward, remember that "Your Final Third" of life is a blank canvas, waiting to be painted with new experiences, adventures, and accomplishments.

Embrace each day with gratitude and intentionality, savoring the moments and cherishing the relationships that enrich your life.

Stay curious, stay engaged, and stay true to yourself as you continue to evolve and thrive in your golden years.

Top 10 Takeaways

1. Reflections on the Journey:

Take a moment to reflect on the journey you have embarked upon throughout the book.

I encourage you to share with your friends and family the insights gained, challenges faced, and milestones achieved along the way.

Pause and appreciate how far you've come in your retirement preparations.

Take a moment to reflect on the transformative journey you have undertaken throughout the book.

Highlight key moments of insight, growth, and resilience that have shaped your retirement preparations.

Reflect now on your personal growth and development throughout the book. I encourage you to celebrate your progress and recognize the resilience and determination you've demonstrated in preparing for retirement.

I congratulate you on the progress made and the challenges overcome and encourage you to continue moving forward with confidence.

2. Words of Encouragement:

Remember it's never too late to make positive changes and that every step forward, no matter how small, brings you closer to your retirement goals.

I encourage you to maintain resilience in the face of setbacks and celebrate the determination and perseverance you've demonstrated thus far.

You have the strength and resourcefulness to overcome any obstacles that may arise on your path to a fulfilling retirement.

Stay committed to your retirement journey, you have the capacity to overcome obstacles and achieve your goals...You've got this!

3. Actionable Takeaways:

Read...Learn...Implement!

Now is the time to take action and create a personalized retirement plan tailored to your circumstances and aspirations.

Summarize the key takeaways from each section of the book and develop actionable steps to implement the advice and strategies discussed.

Break down the key concepts into manageable tasks and prioritize your actions based on your individual circumstances and priorities.

Refer to the checklists & worksheets provided in the Appendix to translate theory into practice and take concrete steps toward your retirement goals.

4. Goal Setting:

I encourage you to set SMART (Specific, Measurable, Achievable, Relevant, Time-bound) goals that align with your values, passions, and priorities.

Whether it's traveling the world, pursuing a lifelong passion, or spending more time with family and friends, articulate your dreams and create a roadmap for turning them into reality.

Dream Big and envision the life you want to lead!

Explore your passions, values, and aspirations. I cannot emphasize enough the importance of setting both short-term and long-term goals and revisiting them regularly to track progress and adjust course as needed.

5. Embracing Change:

Remember the importance of embracing change, the importance of embracing it as an opportunity for growth and renewal and remaining flexible in retirement.

Life is full of unexpected twists and turns, and being open to new opportunities and experiences can lead to greater fulfillment and happiness in Your Final Third.

Change is inevitable, so adopt a mindset of flexibility and adaptability, recognizing that unexpected twists and turns are a natural part of life's journey.

View challenges as opportunities for learning and personal development, rather than obstacles to be feared or avoided.

Explore the transformative power of embracing change and adapting to new circumstances in retirement and develop strategies for managing change effectively and navigating transitions with grace and confidence.

6. Gratitude and Appreciation:

I want to personally thank you for joining me on this journey and for your commitment to preparing for a fulfilling retirement. I encourage you to thank your loved ones, mentors, and advisors who have played a role in shaping your retirement plans for their support.

I encourage you to reflect on the blessings in your life and cultivate an attitude of gratitude for the abundance that surrounds you. Gratitude is a powerful force that can enrich your life and deepen your connections with others.

I suggest implementing a daily written exercise entitled "I am Grateful for _____", listing what you are grateful for each day. Some items may be repetitive, some may seem minor and that's okay, simply write down what comes to your mind.

7. Looking Ahead:

I encourage you to approach this next phase of life with optimism, curiosity, and a sense of adventure, knowing that the best is yet to come.

Envision the life you want to lead and set bold, audacious goals that inspire and motivate you.

Embrace retirement as a time of renewal and reinvention, finding new passions, purpose, and fulfillment.

Explore the endless possibilities that await in Your Final Third.

8. Call to Action:

Now is the time for ACTION!

Take ownership of your retirement journey and continue your quest for lifelong learning and personal growth beyond the pages of this book.

Seek out opportunities for continued learning, growth, and enrichment in retirement, whether through formal education, books, workshops, online courses, volunteer work, or pursuing new hobbies and interests.

Continue to explore topics related to retirement planning, personal development, and holistic well-being and share your experiences and insights with others, to create a community of support and inspiration.

Then, keep seeking out opportunities for continued growth, connection, and contribution in retirement, knowing that the journey is ongoing and full of possibilities.

9. Community Engagement:

I cannot emphasize enough the importance of staying connected with others and being an active participant in your community. Seek out opportunities for social engagement, volunteerism, and meaningful connections that enrich your retirement experience.

When it comes to overall well-being and life satisfaction, the benefits of these experiences are immeasurable, not to mention the positive impact you will make in your local community.

Whether through joining clubs and organizations, attending community events, or volunteering for causes you care about, meaningful relationships and connections with others are essential for cultivating a sense of belonging and purpose in retirement.

10. Final Words for <u>YOUR</u> Final Third:

My wish for you is that you carry this message forward as you embark on the next chapter of your journey...

As you navigate "Your Final Third", embrace each moment with gratitude and purpose.

Remember, it's never too late to chase your dreams, create new memories, and make a difference.

Cherish the **"Go-Go"** years with energy and adventure...

Savor the **"Slow-Go"** years with reflection and connection, and...

Find Peace and Contentment in the **"No-Go"** years.

Life is a journey, and each phase is a precious gift.

Live fully, love deeply, and leave a legacy of joy and wisdom.

"Do not go where the path may lead, go instead where there is no path and leave a trail."

– Ralph Waldo Emerson

Guidance, Tools & Resources

Retirement Ready Assessment

A comprehensive retirement readiness assessment involves evaluating various aspects of your financial, emotional, and physical preparedness for retirement.

Here's a simple assessment to help you determine if you're ready for retirement:

(Rate each section on a scale from 1 (not prepared) to 5 (fully prepared). Add up your scores to see your overall retirement readiness.)

Financial Readiness: Score _____

1. Savings and Investments:

   - Have you calculated how much you'll need for retirement?

   - Do you have enough savings and investments to cover your estimated expenses?

   - Are your investments diversified and aligned with your risk tolerance?

2. Income Sources:

   - Do you have a reliable source of income such as Social Security, pensions, or annuities?

   - Have you determined when you will start taking Social Security benefits to maximize your payments?

3. Expenses:

   - Have you estimated your monthly and annual expenses in retirement, including healthcare, housing, and lifestyle costs?

   - Do you have a budget that accounts for potential inflation and unexpected expenses?

4. Debt:

   - Have you paid off significant debts such as mortgages, car loans, and credit cards?

   - Do you have a plan to manage any remaining debt during retirement?

5. Emergency Fund:

- Do you have an emergency fund that can cover 6-12 months of living expenses?

Healthcare Readiness: Score _____

1. Health Insurance:

   - Are you covered by Medicare or another health insurance plan?

   - Do you understand what Medicare covers and what it doesn't?

2. Long-Term Care:

   - Have you considered long-term care insurance or other plans for potential long-term care needs?

Emotional and Social Readiness: Score _____

1. Purpose and Activities:

- Have you identified hobbies, interests, and activities to keep you engaged and fulfilled?

- Do you have a plan for how you will spend your time and maintain a sense of purpose?

2. Social Connections:

- Do you have a strong social network or plans to stay connected with family and friends?

- Are you involved in community activities or groups that provide social interaction?

Lifestyle Readiness: Score _____

1. Living Arrangements:

   - Have you decided where you will live during retirement? Is your home suitable for aging in place, or do you plan to move?

   - Have you considered the cost of living in your chosen location?

2. Physical Health:

   - Are you maintaining a healthy lifestyle with regular exercise, a balanced diet, and routine medical check-ups?

Legal and Estate Planning: _____

1. Estate Planning:

- Do you have a will, living will, and power of attorney in place?

- Have you reviewed and updated beneficiary designations on your accounts and insurance policies?

2. Tax Planning:

- Are you aware of the tax implications of your retirement income and withdrawals from retirement accounts?

- Have you planned for required minimum distributions (RMDs) from your retirement accounts?

Assessment Summary

Rate each section on a scale from 1 (not prepared) to 5 (fully prepared). Add up your scores to see your overall retirement readiness.

25 points: You are well-prepared for retirement.

18-24 points: You are on the right track but may need to address a few areas.

12-17 points: You have several areas that need attention before you retire.

Below 12 points: Significant planning and adjustments are needed to ensure a secure and fulfilling retirement.

This assessment should give you a clearer picture of your readiness for retirement and highlight areas that may require further attention or planning.

The following tools, worksheets, and guides complement the content of this book and provide you with practical resources to apply the information to your own life.

Many of these resources can be created using basic software programs like Microsoft Excel or Word, or they may be available through reputable websites like seniorsolutionstoday.com, government agencies, or non-profit organizations specializing in retirement and senior issues.

Exercise and Activity Log to track your physical activity and exercise routines.

Smart Goal Setting Worksheet to help you set and track personal development goals, such as learning new skills or pursuing hobbies.

A Wellness Checklist of activities and habits for you to incorporate into your daily routines.

Retirement Saving Calculator to help you estimate your retirement savings needs based on your lifestyle and goals.

Budgeting Worksheet to track your income, expenses, and savings goals.

Investment Risk Assessment to help you assess your risk tolerance and align your investment strategy with your financial goals.

Social Security Benefit Estimator tool on the Social Security Administration's website to help you estimate your Social Security benefits based on different claiming scenarios or for a more accurate optimized report *contact us at seniorsolutionstoday.com.*

Medicare Enrollment Checklist outlining the steps for enrolling in Medicare, including deadlines and important documents needed. *Contact us at seniorsolutionstoday.com*

Medicare Coverage Comparison Chart of different Medicare coverage options (e.g., Original Medicare vs. Medicare Advantage) to help readers understand their choices. *Contact us at seniorsolutionstoday.com.*

Home Inventory Worksheet to inventory belongings and determine what to keep, donate, or sell when downsizing.

Moving Checklist/Timeline to help you plan and organize your move, including tasks such as packing, hiring movers, and updating addresses.

Neighborhood Research Guide to help you research and evaluate potential relocation destinations, including factors such as cost of living, amenities, and healthcare facilities.

Estate Planning Worksheet provides essential estate planning documents, such as wills, trusts, and powers of attorney, along with guidance on how to create and update them.

The Executor Duties Guide outlines the responsibilities of an executor or personal representative, including estate administration tasks and legal obligations.

Advance Directives Template to create your advance directive, including instructions for medical care and appointing a healthcare proxy.

Social Engagement Calendar to help you schedule social activities and events, such as club meetings, volunteer opportunities, and social outings.

Community Resource Directory of local resources and organizations that offer social activities, support services, and volunteer opportunities for seniors.

Networking Worksheet to help you identify and cultivate new social connections, including strategies for meeting people and building relationships.

Should you need assistance or have any questions about any of these resources, feel free to contact me at:

www.seniorsolutionstoday.com

Glossary

Section I: Personal Development & Fitness

Cognitive Decline

The gradual loss of cognitive abilities, including memory, reasoning, and attention, often associated with aging.

Functional Fitness

Exercises and activities that focus on improving strength, flexibility, and mobility for everyday tasks and movements, such as walking, lifting, and bending.

Healthy Aging

The process of maintaining physical, mental, and emotional well-being as one grows older, often through lifestyle choices such as diet, exercise, and social engagement.

Mindfulness

The practice of being fully present and engaged in the present moment, often cultivated through meditation and mindfulness exercises to reduce stress and enhance well-being.

Nutrient-Dense Foods

Foods that provide a high amount of nutrients relative to their calorie content, such as fruits, vegetables, lean proteins, and whole grains.

Strength Training

Physical exercises that focus on building muscle strength and endurance, often involving resistance training with weights, resistance bands, or bodyweight exercises.

Section II: Financial Planning

401(k) Plan

An employer-sponsored retirement savings plan that allows employees to contribute a portion of their pre-tax income to a retirement account, often with employer matching contributions.

Annuity

A financial product that provides a guaranteed stream of income for a specified period or for life, often purchased from an insurance company.

Asset Allocation

The distribution of investment assets across different asset classes, such as stocks, bonds, and cash equivalents, to achieve a desired risk-return profile.

Compound Interest

The process by which interest is added to the principal sum of an investment, and then interest is earned on both the original principal and the accumulated interest.

Diversification

A risk management strategy that involves spreading investments across different asset classes, sectors, or geographic regions to reduce exposure to any single investment or risk.

Inflation

The rate at which the general level of prices for goods and services rises over time, eroding the purchasing power of money.

IRA (Individual Retirement Account)

A tax-advantaged retirement account that allows individuals to save for retirement by investing in stocks, bonds, and other assets.

Life Insurance Retirement Plan (LIRP)

A permanent life insurance policy that can help you save for retirement. LIRPs have a cash value component that grows tax-deferred over time at a predetermined interest, you can withdraw or borrow funds.

Long-Term Care Insurance

Insurance coverage that helps cover the costs of long-term care services, such as nursing home care, assisted living, and home healthcare, not typically covered by health insurance or Medicare.

Required Minimum Distribution (RMD)

The minimum amount that individuals with tax-deferred retirement accounts, such as Traditional IRAs and 401(k) plans, must withdraw annually after reaching a certain age (usually 72-75 based on birth year) to avoid penalties.

Risk Tolerance

An individual's willingness and ability to tolerate fluctuations in the value of their investments or accept the possibility of investment losses.

Tax-Deferred Account

An investment account, such as a Traditional IRA or 401(k), in which taxes on contributions and earnings are deferred until withdrawals are made in retirement.

Section III: Navigating Social Security & Medicare

Income-Related Monthly Adjustment Amount (IRMAA)

As additional charge that some Medicare enrollees pay each month if their income is above a certain level.

Medicaid

A joint federal and state program that provides health coverage to low-income individuals and families, including certain elderly and disabled individuals who meet eligibility requirements beyond those covered by Medicare.

Medicare Advantage Plan

Also known as Medicare Part C, these are private health plans that provide Medicare benefits to beneficiaries. They often include additional benefits beyond what Original Medicare offers, such as vision, dental, and prescription drug coverage.

Medicare Part D

The part of Medicare that provides prescription drug coverage. Medicare Part D plans are offered by private insurance companies approved by

Medicare and help beneficiaries pay for the cost of prescription drugs.

Medicare Supplement Insurance (Medigap)

A type of private insurance policy that helps fill in the gaps in coverage left by Original Medicare, such as copayments, coinsurance, and deductibles. Medigap policies are sold by private insurance companies and are standardized by the federal government.

Social Security Administration (SSA)

The federal agency that is responsible for administering Social Security programs, including retirement, disability, and survivors' benefits. The SSA also oversees the issuance of Social Security numbers and maintains earnings records for workers.

Social Security Disability Insurance (SSDI)

A federal program that provides benefits to individuals who are unable to work due to a qualifying disability. SSDI benefits are based on the individual's work history and earnings.

Social Security Full Retirement Age (FRA)

The age at which individuals are eligible to receive full Social Security retirement benefits. FRA varies depending on the year of birth, ranging from 65 to 67 years old.

Section IV: Real Estate Downsizing & Relocation

Downsizing

The process of moving to a smaller home or living space, often undertaken by retirees to reduce expenses, simplify their lifestyle, or accommodate changing needs.

Closing Costs

The fees and expenses associated with completing a real estate transaction, including loan origination fees, appraisal fees, title insurance, and escrow fees.

Home Equity

The value of a homeowner's interest in their home, calculated by subtracting the outstanding mortgage balance from the home's market value.

Homeowners Association (HOA)

An organization within a residential community that establishes and enforces rules and regulations, collects fees from homeowners, and manages common areas and amenities.

Relocation Specialist

A professional who assists individuals and families with the logistical and emotional aspects of moving to a new home or location, providing support with packing, moving logistics, and settling into a new community.

Section V: Legal Documents & Estate Planning

Advance Directive

A legal document that specifies an individual's preferences for medical treatment and healthcare decisions in the event they become unable to communicate or make decisions for themselves.

Beneficiary

An individual or entity designated to receive assets or benefits from a will, trust, insurance policy, retirement account, or other financial instrument upon the death of the account holder or policyholder.

Estate Planning

The process of arranging for the distribution of one's assets and the management of their affairs after death, typically through the use of wills, trusts, and other legal documents.

Living Will

A legal document that outlines an individual's preferences for medical treatment and end-of-life care in the event they are unable to communicate their wishes.

Probate

The legal process of administering the estate of a deceased person, including validating their will, paying debts, and distributing assets to beneficiaries.

Section VI: Embracing Community & Social Connections

Civic Engagement

Active participation in the democratic process and community affairs, such as voting, attending town hall meetings, or advocating for social causes, to contribute to positive change and strengthen civil society.

Community Engagement

Involvement in activities or organizations within one's community, such as volunteering, attending events, or joining clubs, to foster connections with others and contribute to the well-being of the community.

Digital Literacy

The ability to effectively use digital technologies, such as computers, smartphones, and the internet, to communicate, access information, and participate in online social networks and communities.

Intergenerational Connections

Relationships and interactions between individuals of different generations, such as grandparents and grandchildren, which can provide mutual benefits, including wisdom-sharing, companionship, and a sense of belonging.

Loneliness

The subjective feeling of being alone or lacking meaningful social connections, which can have negative effects on mental and physical health, particularly among older adults.

Social Capital

The collective value of social networks, relationships, and interactions within a community, which can lead to increased trust, cooperation, and reciprocity among individuals and groups.

Social Isolation

The lack of social contact or meaningful connections with others, which can lead to feelings of loneliness and negatively impact mental and physical health.

Social Support Network

A group of family, friends, neighbors, or other individuals who provide emotional, practical, and sometimes financial support during times of need or challenge.

Social Prescribing

An approach to healthcare that involves connecting patients with non-medical community resources and activities, such as support groups, exercise classes, or arts programs, to improve overall well-being and address social determinants of health.

Volunteerism

The act of donating one's time, skills, or resources to a cause or organization without expecting monetary compensation, often with the goal of making a positive impact on the community or society.

Suggested Reading

Financial Planning and Retirement

These books cover a wide range of topics related to financial planning and retirement, from investment strategies and budgeting to navigating healthcare and achieving financial independence.

1. **The Simple Path To Wealth: Your Road Map To Financial Independence And A Rich, Free Life** by JL Collins – This book offers straightforward advice on investing and building wealth, emphasizing the importance of financial independence.

2. **Your Money or Your Life: 9 Steps to Transforming Your Relationship with Money and Achieving Financial Independence** by Vicki Robin and Joe Dominguez – A classic guide to financial planning that focuses on aligning your spending with your values to achieve financial freedom.

3. **The Bogleheads' Guide to Retirement Planning** by Taylor Larimore, Mel Lindauer, Richard A. Ferri, and Laura F. Dogu – Written by a group of financial experts who follow the investment principles of John C. Bogle, this book provides comprehensive advice on planning for retirement.

4. **How to Make Your Money Last: The Indispensable Retirement Guide** by Jane Bryant Quinn – This guide offers practical advice on managing your finances in retirement to ensure your money lasts as long as you do.

5. **Retire Inspired: It's Not an Age, It's a Financial Number** by Chris Hogan – Hogan encourages readers to think differently about retirement and provides strategies for saving and investing to achieve a comfortable retirement.

6. **The New Retirementality: Planning Your Life and Living Your Dreams...at Any Age You Want** by Mitch Anthony – This book challenges traditional notions of retirement and encourages readers to create a retirement plan that reflects their personal goals and desires.

7. **The Retirement Maze: What You Should Know Before and After You Retire** by Rob Pascale, Louis H. Primavera, and Rip Roach – This book explores the psychological and emotional aspects of retirement, offering advice on how to navigate the transition successfully.

8. **Get What's Yours for Medicare: Maximize Your Coverage, Minimize Your Costs** by Philip Moeller – A practical guide to understanding Medicare and making the most of your coverage.

9. **Can I Retire Yet? How to Make the Biggest Financial Decision of the Rest of Your Life** by Darrow Kirkpatrick – This book provides a step-by-step approach to determining if you have enough money to retire and how to plan for a secure retirement.

10. **Smart Women Finish Rich: 9 Steps to Achieving Financial Security and Funding Your Dreams** by David Bach – A financial planning guide tailored to women, offering strategies for saving, investing, and planning for retirement.

Health & Wellness

These books offer a wealth of knowledge and practical tips for maintaining health and wellness as we age, covering everything from physical fitness and nutrition to mental health and emotional well-being.

1. **Younger Next Year: Live Strong, Fit, and Sexy - Until You're 80 and Beyond** by Chris Crowley and Henry S. Lodge M.D. – This book offers a comprehensive guide to healthy aging, focusing on exercise, nutrition, and mental health.

2. **The Blue Zones Solution: Eating and Living Like the World's Healthiest People** by Dan Buettner – Buettner explores the lifestyles and diets of the world's longest-lived people and provides actionable advice for adopting these habits.

3. **Aging Well: Surprising Guideposts to a Happier Life from the Landmark Harvard Study of Adult Development** by George E. Vaillant – Drawing on decades of research, this book offers insights into the factors that contribute to a fulfilling and healthy old age.

4. **The Gift of Years: Growing Older Gracefully** by Joan Chittister – A thoughtful reflection on the spiritual and emotional aspects of aging, emphasizing the importance of finding purpose and joy in later life.

5. **The Longevity Paradox: How to Die Young at a Ripe Old Age** by Dr. Steven R. Gundry – Gundry offers a program for improving health and longevity, focusing on diet, exercise, and lifestyle changes.

6. **The End of Alzheimer's: The First Program to Prevent and Reverse Cognitive Decline** by Dale Bredesen – This book presents a groundbreaking approach to preventing and treating Alzheimer's disease, based on cutting-edge research.

7. **The 30-Day Alzheimer's Solution: The Definitive Food and Lifestyle Guide to Preventing Cognitive Decline** by Dean Sherzai and Ayesha Sherzai – A practical guide to reducing the risk of Alzheimer's through diet and lifestyle changes.

8. **Keep Sharp: Build a Better Brain at Any Age** by Sanjay Gupta – Dr. Gupta offers evidence-based strategies for maintaining and improving brain health throughout life.

9. **Strong Women Stay Young** by Miriam E. Nelson – This book focuses on the benefits of strength training for women, providing exercises and routines to maintain muscle mass and bone density as we age.

10. **Ageless Soul: The Lifelong Journey Toward Meaning and Joy** by Thomas Moore – Moore explores the spiritual and emotional dimensions of aging, encouraging readers to find meaning and fulfillment in their later years.

11. **Healthy Aging: A Lifelong Guide to Your Well-Being** by Andrew Weil, M.D. – Dr. Weil offers a holistic approach to healthy aging, including advice on diet, exercise, and mental wellness.

12. **The Complete Guide to Healthy Aging: A Self-Care Manual** by Gary Small, M.D. – This guide provides comprehensive advice on various aspects of aging, from physical health and nutrition to mental well-being and social connections.

Personal Growth and Inspiration

These books offer a wealth of wisdom, inspiration, and practical advice for those seeking personal growth and fulfillment in their later years.

1. **The Second Mountain: The Quest for a Moral Life** by David Brooks – Brooks explores the idea that the first mountain in life is about personal achievement, while the second mountain is about finding deeper meaning through relationships and commitments.

2. **Man's Search for Meaning** by Viktor E. Frankl – A profound exploration of finding purpose and meaning in life, even in the face of suffering, based on Frankl's experiences in a Nazi concentration camp.

3. **The Power of Now: A Guide to Spiritual Enlightenment** by Eckhart Tolle – Tolle encourages readers to live in the present moment and find spiritual growth and fulfillment.

4. **The Four Agreements: A Practical Guide to Personal Freedom** by Don Miguel Ruiz – A transformative book that offers simple yet profound principles for achieving personal freedom and living a fulfilling life.

5. **The Gifts of Imperfection: Let Go of Who You Think You're Supposed to Be and Embrace Who You Are** by Brené Brown – Brown's work on embracing vulnerability and living authentically is inspiring and empowering.

6. **Rising Strong: How the Ability to Reset Transforms the Way We Live, Love, Parent, and Lead** by Brené Brown – Another powerful book by Brown, focusing on the process of rising after setbacks and challenges.

7. **The Artist's Way: A Spiritual Path to Higher Creativity** by Julia Cameron – A classic guide to unlocking creativity and personal growth through various exercises and practices.

8. **Daring Greatly: How the Courage to Be Vulnerable Transforms the Way We Live, Love, Parent, and Lead** by Brené Brown – This book explores the power of vulnerability and its role in personal and professional growth.

9. **Big Magic: Creative Living Beyond Fear** by Elizabeth Gilbert – Gilbert shares her insights on creativity and encourages readers to embrace their curiosity and passion.

10. **The Alchemist** by Paulo Coelho – A beloved novel that inspires readers to follow their dreams and listen to their hearts.

11. **Awaken the Giant Within: How to Take Immediate Control of Your Mental, Emotional, Physical and Financial Destiny!** by Tony Robbins – Robbins provides strategies and tools for achieving personal and professional goals.

12. **The Wisdom of Sundays: Life-Changing Insights from Super Soul Conversations** by Oprah Winfrey – A collection of inspirational conversations with thought leaders and visionaries, offering insights on personal growth and spirituality.

13. **The Untethered Soul: The Journey Beyond Yourself** by Michael A. Singer – Singer offers a guide to spiritual growth and enlightenment, encouraging readers to free themselves from limiting thoughts and emotions.

14. **Atomic Habits: An Easy & Proven Way to Build Good Habits & Break Bad Ones** by James Clear – Clear's book provides practical advice for creating positive habits and making small changes that lead to significant personal growth.

15. **The Road Back to You: An Enneagram Journey to Self-Discovery** by Ian Morgan Cron and Suzanne Stabile – This book explores the Enneagram, a powerful tool for understanding oneself and fostering personal growth.

Lifestyle & Leisure

These books provide a variety of ideas and inspirations for enhancing lifestyle and leisure, from cooking and decluttering to travel and creative pursuits.

1. **A Man Called Ove** by Fredrik Backman – A heartwarming novel about finding friendship and purpose in the later years of life.

2. **A Year in Provence** by Peter Mayle – A delightful memoir about the author's experience moving to the French countryside and embracing a new way of life.

3. **The Little Paris Bookshop** by Nina George – A novel that explores the healing power of books and the adventure of setting sail for a new chapter in life.

4. **The Art of Stillness: Adventures in Going Nowhere** by Pico Iyer – Iyer examines the benefits of slowing down and finding peace in stillness.

5. **The Joy of Less: A Minimalist Guide to Declutter, Organize, and Simplify** by Francine Jay – A guide to embracing a minimalist lifestyle, focusing on the joys of living with less.

6. **The Book of Joy: Lasting Happiness in a Changing World** by Dalai Lama and Desmond Tutu – Two spiritual leaders share their insights on finding joy and happiness in life.

7. **The Life-Changing Magic of Tidying Up: The Japanese Art of Decluttering and Organizing** by Marie Kondo – Kondo's approach to decluttering can help create a more serene and enjoyable living space.

8. **Eat Pray Love: One Woman's Search for Everything Across Italy, India and Indonesia** by Elizabeth Gilbert – A memoir about self-discovery and finding pleasure in life's adventures.

9. **The Joy of Cooking** by Irma S. Rombauer, Marion Rombauer Becker, and Ethan Becker – A classic cookbook that can bring joy and creativity to the kitchen.

10. **In the Company of Women: Inspiration and Advice from over 100 Makers, Artists, and Entrepreneurs** by Grace Bonney – A collection of interviews with creative women who share their stories and advice on living a fulfilling life.

11. **The Art of Travel** by Alain de Botton – De Botton explores the pleasures and insights that travel can bring to our lives.

12. **How to Retire Happy, Wild, and Free: Retirement Wisdom That You Won't Get from Your Financial Advisor** by Ernie J. Zelinski – This book focuses on the non-financial aspects of retirement, offering advice on creating a fulfilling and enjoyable post-work life.

13. **Knitting for Peace: Make the World a Better Place One Stitch at a Time** by Betty Christiansen – A book that combines the joy of knitting with the satisfaction of helping others.

14. **The Great Outdoors: A User's Guide** by Brendan Leonard – A practical and inspirational guide to enjoying outdoor activities and adventures.

15. **Birding Without Borders: An Obsession, a Quest, and the Biggest Year in the World** by Noah Strycker – A memoir about the author's year-long quest to see as many bird species as possible, offering insights into the joys of birdwatching.

16. **The Art of Mindful Living: How to Bring Love, Compassion, and Inner Peace into Your Daily Life** by Thich Nhat Hanh – A guide to incorporating mindfulness into everyday activities for a more peaceful and joyful life.

Biographies and Memoirs

These books provide a range of perspectives and insights that can help you contemplate and appreciate the various stages of life, particularly "Your Final Third".

1. **Being Mortal: Medicine and What Matters in the End** by Atul Gawande – A profound exploration of aging, death, and the quality of life in our later years.

2. **Tuesdays with Morrie** by Mitch Albom – A touching memoir about the author's conversations with his former college professor,

Morrie Schwartz, who shares wisdom about living a meaningful life.

3. **The Measure of My Days** by Florida Scott-Maxwell – A candid and insightful diary of an 85-year-old woman reflecting on her life, aging, and the human condition.

4. **The Last Lecture** by Randy Pausch – A moving memoir by a professor who, after being diagnosed with terminal cancer, shares his life lessons and advice for living life to the fullest.

5. **When Breath Becomes Air** by Paul Kalanithi – A poignant memoir by a neurosurgeon facing terminal cancer, reflecting on his life, career, and what it means to live a meaningful life.

6. **A Long Way Home** by Saroo Brierley – The memoir of a man who, after being lost in India as a child and adopted by an Australian family, embarks on a journey to find his birth family.

7. **Educated** by Tara Westover – A powerful memoir about a woman who grows up in a strict and abusive household in rural Idaho but

eventually escapes to learn about the wider world through education.

8. **The Art of Aging: A Doctor's Prescription for Well-Being** by Sherwin B. Nuland – A thoughtful exploration of how to age gracefully and maintain physical and mental health.

9. **I Remember Nothing and Other Reflections** by Nora Ephron – A collection of witty and poignant essays by the late writer and filmmaker, reflecting on aging, memory, and life.

10. **My Beloved World** by Sonia Sotomayor – An inspiring memoir by the first Latina Supreme Court Justice, detailing her journey from a Bronx housing project to the federal bench.

Made in the USA
Middletown, DE
07 December 2024

66337852R00133